AF333973

THE REFILLABLE STEAMY

BY

THE BABYLON THEATRE

LITMUS

Printed in the United States of America by
C. S. Crowther at Folk Frog Press.

This project is supported by a grant from the National
Endowment for the Arts in Washington D.C., a federal
agency.

Patricia Kingsbury -- front cover
Kim Babylon Long -- inside photography
Peter Dustrud -- back cover photo

A Litmus First Edition
Litmus Library Card 76-17-29

Library of Congress Card Number 76-21596

Stewart, Greg, & Palmer, Nolan
       The Refillable Steamy

The Babylon Theatre
ISBN 0-915214-17-2

LITMUS INC.
574 3rd Avenue
Salt Lake City Utah 84103

Come to where your tongue's fallin' out!

follow your lungs to where you're

creatin' a havoc zone.   Feel

the corridors of your brain surge

with the evil of the stuff.

Don't it feel nice?   Feel that

smoke travel?   feel it come

out your eyes?   feel it

filter into your brain feel it

come down your lungs feel it

surge into the tube?

Picture the cat as he takes

the smoke into his lungs

fries his brain and never

asks why.

INGREDIENTS

black coffee added as a stablizer

artificial color may have been added

some settling of contents

has already occured

ABRIDGED HISTORY OF BABYLON

We used to sit around and babble to each other. It was the best entertainment we had when we were living together. We found language was becoming hard just like the world we had seen once in a science-fiction jam and we tried to soften it up. It was easy. Babbling released taboo verbal elements and gave us comedy, then hysteria, then burn out. Gradually we wanted to eliminate the burn and about 9 months later Babylon was born. Or reborn. After all we had just come together not been created together. Our separate adverse reactions to life as we knew it had drawn us together.

Where now? Language is something from nothing, a real human creation. Godlike we command it not from fear but with humor. If it doesnt give itself freely, to hell with it! Words are all we own. We wanted to open a refreshment stand for words. To turn the lights on this flow of personal description.

And yet we were led directly almost unwillingly to the extreme presence of one great paradoxical Prime Law of Babylon: 'People will believe that for which no alternative is allowed.'

So, we thought, let us carry on with the language of our birth as though it could carry us right on through. We are not here, we are on our way there, and still at this point we only talk to each other, thoughts being separate like stars, no help from the other only the vague image of flat being. Expect alternatives and you can live like a king. Accept no alternatives and you can only be led along, no doubt dragging your heels all the while.

Babylon was and is a starting place. Set to go, we cannot imagine stopping. Well, we could, but . . . something out of nothing is always our greatest dream.

'The Dreams of Philip the Snorter' was first produced in 1973 as part of a live show titled 'Burnt Organy Cherries' performed at Westminster College, Salt Lake City, in the fall of that year and again in the spring of 1974. We disguised ourselves as the World Warp Theatre.

'I Dont Want the Rice to Knock Me Down' was written for and first performed at the Underwater Poetry Festival held in SLC in 1974, sponsored by Litmus Inc. During the winter of 74-75 we recorded it in sound. Charlie Potts appeared with us in this recording.

'The Defendant' was emitted by Palmer, Potts & Stewart onto tape one day in 73 and later transcribed. Babylon is solely responsible for its contents. Any requests for grammar checks may be so addressed.

'Pilgrim's Problems' was written in April 1975 as our contribution to the bicentennial, though really a counter-proposal. It was first recorded and aired at KUER-FM, University of Utah, that month. Later it was included in the live show 'Sonar and Yet So Fear' produced in June 1975 by Babylon Theatre.

'The DOA Squack Show' is composed of material created over a period of 5 years and finally arranged into the live production 'Sonar and Yet So Fear' which was sponsored by the Human Ensemble and presented in their Glass Factory theatre in SLC. Late in 75 it was produced on videotape (condensed to one half-hour) at ITV, University of Utah; Jack Vetterli, Director, for cable tv transmission.

'Walking On The Feet of The Faithful' was written in early 1976 as prototype of a proposed radio series. Its true manifestation is yet to appear.

anhistoric play

characters:

A. J. K. Waterbottomly, series host
Phillip the Snorter, King of Regurge
his **Son**
Ernestine; counsellor, monk, and wife to Philip,
    and secret leader of the Turks.
a **Messenger**
Charles of Horn, a confused war hero
peasants
minstrels

setting:

Prime Time

ACT I

(Baroque music)

A.J.K.:   And welcome back again to section 7 part 3 verse 6 of "The Dreams of Phillip the Snorter." As you will remember from our last episode, Phillip had just recompensed and acompensated the Turkish army for loss of several hundred turkeys which they had encumbered while crossing his river--his river which ran under the gate and through the barbed wire fence, leading to the tunnel wherein Phillip kept his mortuary, his obituary, and his monk of several colors, Ernestine. As we join the cast now, the king is gloriously snoring in his bedroom, where he is about to be awakened by the rising sun.

Phillip: Yip-ha, yip-ha, yip-ha, yip-ha. . .

Son: *(entering)* Father, Father, wake up! It is I, the rising son.

Phil: Good night! it's morning!

Son: And I've risen this morning to give you the first piece of advice.

Phil: Tell me my son, is it your custom to come customing around, finding your own recompense in the pockets of my shirt-pants?

Son: My dear father, my slippers I left in the closet of the maid . . . I had to walk barefoot.

Phil: Very well, state your business and then find me a cocktail.

Son: It's about Ernestine.

Phil: Is that the same Ernestine that I married?

Son: Father, I deign to call him mother though monk and teacher both she be.

Phil: And well loved mistress she to me.

Son: But Father, I object to her keeping those turkeys in the tunnel; their stench piles on itself till when she lifts the upper door it rushes into my room which lies just above and drives me out with the smell up my nose. Her well-colored face has shined in every room and closet and laughs at servant and rat alike, but cant these turkeys be made out of the tunnel and into a profit for us?

Phil: Well I've been trying this for several weeks, but the very turkeys which we onslaught overtook from those Turkish raiding parties, were the very subsistence level that they were expecting. Now, we're not required to own up to them any more than our forthright share or the fifth right land profit of the seventh factory. So, if you can replace these turkeys in a matter of, oh, a nickel a pound, we could scalp them and feed them to the Turks.

Son: Father, you know as well as I do that the Turks are not warbound and in fact are not even peacebound. These Turks are obviously nothing but a drunken hunting party, not bound to trouble us.

Phil: No, the Turks indeed are bound!

Son: Oh--

Phil: We have 24 Turks in the backroom closet.

Son: Sir!--

Phil: 36 were found outside our gate groveling in the bean patch, looking for me.

Son: Speak you of those featherless clucks that I found dipping in the ointment of the repository?

Phil: Oh, the very same, my boy.

Son: Father, your glorious attitude is rectal to my needs.
           Now, back to that tunnel--that windbag of glory--
           Ernestine.

Phil: Oh yes.

Son: I mean to say that she is--

Phil: Well she's such a silly old biddy-- *(a knock from
           without)* --oh, excuse me, Edw--Hen--my son.
           (exit son)
           Come in, uhem, your majesty awaits thy humble counsel,
           crounsel, and crawl at my knees. Yes constable.

Ernestine: *(entering)* Milord, it is I, your trusted monk-e-wrench.
           I've just been crawling in the deepest cellars and I
           noticed a slight variance in the quality of the wine.
           You were having wine, I suppose with breakfast?
           I wanted to warn you that number C is not quite ready.
           Well. . . it's been spilled.

Phil: Thank you, monk. You know how little I've respected
           your courage for all these years and your confidence
           is simply not a good credit rating, however--

Ern: O dominic, dominic, saltpeter and acid. . .

Phil: Ah, I can see you havent lost your religious gurgor.

Ern: Nagh. . .

Phil: Thank you, monkey. . .

Ern: Now I'm going to show you--

Phil: Now about Ernestine. . .

Ern: Ha ha. Milord, have your forgotten your glasses?

Phil: Oh, Ernestine. . .

Ern: Ha ha ha.

Phil: You go by so many names it's hard to know when you're
           coming. . . How are things going at the school? Oh,
           that's a pious mask you have there.

Ern: This mask was painted by several students strained by
           me. I'm training a class right now. I gave them an
           assignment to paint your face, and I was wondering if--

Phil: Oh please, dont let them touch me my acne is so touchy,
           you know, oh please. . .

Ern: Oh, they wont usually want to . . .

Phil: Now as you were saying of this wine.

Ern: Oh, the wine.

Phil: Have you tried it?

Ern: Yes I have, I drank a small bottle of it but the stuff
        is rancid. There are several casks of it which are
        simply green with envy. I dont mean to say that it's
        too old, mind you, I mean to say that it's not old enough.

Phil: So you suppose that this means great double treachery
        for me?

Ern: Milord. May I speak to you honestly?

Phil: Oh, I wish you would. It's been such a long time
        since I've ever--

Ern: Milord. Milord. There are rumors about the castle that
        several of the members of your crounsel have been
        speaking rather openly in the last days. I want to
        assure you, milord, that I dont believe a word of it
        but dont you think you ought to make some sort of
        oath or perpetual swear over this. . . this. . . mouthing
        off has gone right into the village.

Phil: In this. . . in this it is no. . . no secret in this kingdom
        of ours that I am the largest member--uh, stockholder
        we have. I'm not required to wear pants when I bathe,
        and well, my cheerleaders are among the highest caring
        stock--wolves and dogs--we've kept in the kingdom corral.
        (a knock)
        Ernestine, I seem to be--

Ern: Excuse me, I think this is my man. . . thank you.
        Here we are. It was my man. He brought you a sample.

Phil: I never knew you had a man, Ernestine.

Ern: Oh milord. . . please, milord. . .

Phil: I know I am. All you need to do is get on your knees.

Ern: I've brought you a sample of the wine which I'd like
        you to try before serving it to the guests. If you'd
        just take a sip, because you see the leaves are still
        floating in it.

Phil: Oh, Ernestine, could you possibly, uh, try it first?

Ern: Milord, trust you me not?

Phil: You said there were several overt members hanging around
        in the halls, and who knows but what your man has
        stunk upon these tremulous faws. He could himself
        be stuck in the rear, found floating in the moat.

Ern: (examining bottle) Milord, speak you not of such

fouled wine, for I fear that my man has brought
the wrong bottle.

Phil: Not C Keg?

Ern: This is the good wine of which I have spoken so
enviously in days past. This is the wine that has
laid me out on a couch several times in the last week!

Phil: You say that, when I was there, but atop your buttocks?

Ern: Drink you this wine, and spill not evermore such
glib snidery.

Phil: Then, to your health, and your barrenity.

Ern: Yes, and to the banality of all turkeys.
(they drink)

Phil: Ah, I see what you mean. Already the room begin to
float around my head. . .

Ern: Yes, the venom which floats through my cumbering
ears gives me. . . snake eyes. . .

Phil: Snake eyes?

Ern: Shall we dance?

Phil: Oh, let us dance.

Ern: Your honor. . .
(they dance. crowd noises are heard outside.)

Phil: Ernestine, I hear my subjects roosting under our window
and crawling up my vine. I'll step to the balcony and
give them a line. *(goes to balcony)*
Plebes: My faithful monk and loyal mascot to the
Snorters, Ernestine, tells me and my galloping son
confirms there's distemper here for me. But now we
must stipple selfish anger and turn straight to a
matter of personal ineptitude--the Turks. My
many-hued monk bids we drink and raises me 3 to
fight. We must swish this dribble out of our land. The
turks are gobbling us up and this snorting court wants
fun! We rise and need bread, locate our lock-stock-
and-future in the barrel company, with a fast aim for
peace. Will Great Gob make turkeys of us all? Nay
nay--for I, Phillip *(snort)* will lead to the bar and buy
a bottle for the bravest man the army ever spawned--
me! and for the winners of our glorious war!
(exeunt)

(in the Turkish camp outside the city. Some minstrels cross, singing.)

Minstrels:

Philip rode out with a bottle in hand,
leading his army across the sand.
Fa la la la la la la.
But as the 2 armies clashed in the fray
Phillip sat off and drank in the hay.
Fa la la la la la la.
When the smoke cleared and the fight was done,
Phillip lay baking in the sun
He had led no charge as a king should do,

And the only sword slice was aimed at
the meat for the stew.
Fa la la la la la la la la la la la
la la la la la!

(minstrels exit. a messenger enters and approaches Ernestine, secret leader of the Turks.)

Messenger: My lord, the King, Phillip the Regurgitator, sends his quiet admiration to your high heels, but-- since the turkeys which he has so oft kept in his vinyard have been forthright destroyed, barely stuck up by our lances and swords, he feels it a must that you come to him.

Ern: I dont feel that I am required to spend money for this venture; does your lord not send some liege or leach?

Mess: My lady, we've tried to get him to stop leaching, but you know Phillip, he regurgitates as fast as he slaws.

1st Peasant: That snorting nose has been seen in twelve bottles on the same night--farther out than any of his servants.

Mess: He speaks the truth my lady. He . . . follows *me* where I go.

Ern: Yes, Phillip is such a wart. We'll decide this matter later. Come you, servant, and attend me to my tent. *(exit)*

2nd peas: Phillip's warts may soon spread to our camp. I myself have seen his ladyship riding toward the city as the midnight guard was falling down on duty.

3rd peas: Aye, and Phillip's drunks are a holy mess. It is **said**
he sat off his horse while riding into battle.
(enter Charles)

Charles: *(battle-shocked)* Unhhhhh . . . That snorting nose has
drunk too far. . .

1st peas: Who are you?

Chas: I be Charles, redundant head of the family Horn.
And I bring no news but bad news. . . for Phillip!
This shield on which I hold a bloody tomb has
bespake me greatly in battle!

Mess: Oh my lord, is this not the shield of King Phillip
of Regurge?

Chas: It is! The snorting nose has bowed his last.
I have sliced it, ha ha!

Mess: Where have you found yon shield, following in the
fallow of the field?

Chas: This shield picked me up from the bleeding field
of the wine-soaked king, and I bled him. . . I bled
him until he released my hand, and my hand was
picked up by this shield which picked me up and
carried me to this kingdom. I, Charles of Hornicast,
being begot by several of the finest members of the
royal line, I bespeak thee my lord--er, my messenger,
to entreat me to a compassing food, a dinner worth
remembering!

Mess: Excuse me, I'll report these circumstances to my lady.
(he enters Ernestine's tent.)
My lady, my lady, my lord. . . my lord, my lady. . .
please, wake up.

Ern: Speak easy, speak easy, I'm quite aware.

Mess: Yes, I feel my tongue is getting numb and thick. . .

Ern: Speak you what you think, servant, and man you not
to with too many words.

Mess: My lady, Charles of Horn was just here; in fact
now bathes in yon sudsy temple fountain.

Ern: Speak you of the Horncaster which has been plundering
the southern quarters?

Mess: The one who now comes upon his back with his shield
in bloody hand on bloody wrist, and says of his
torment with the King my Phillip.

Ern: What? Speak you of Phillip? What news, what news?

Mess: Only that the battle is in some stagnant state, and that none there live nor even fight. Some of them have been found making love in the back of the haystacks. But Phillip, whose righteous gurgor has held in quell almighty surgent monstrils, now lies pale and droll. . . stuck.

Ern: Huh--Phillip?. . . *Stuck?*

Mess: Indeed my lady such tremulous news I hail to bring you since it hail outside with rain and sleety snow.

Ern: Tell me, is this Charles, the Horncaster, responsible?

Mess: Not very madam, but none the less he holds in Phillip's hands his grubby shield.

Ern: He brought Phillip's hands too? And his famous nose I hope?

Mess: Oh , no. . .

Ern: I've wanted that nose for my trophy room for years.

Mess: This Charles. . . makes static remarks as though his radio were ablink, his eyes flashing with the indigenous quell of lusty fervor. Indeed, those hands have done him nought but wrong.

Ern: Ha! Speak you no more. Go now and to the tent of Charles this demon caster and send him forthright to my humble abode. I would speak with him in earnest quest.

Mess: Yes.

Ern: And after you've done that stop off at the trough and get a wash, your face is ugly.

Mess: Yes. . . ma'am.
(he exits and enters the tent of Charles)
Charles, Charles! Aha. My lady speaks that I would want with you.

Charles: What speak you language, son?

Mess: Upon the message that I had seen the King's in bloody hand shielded, she requests your presence and your penance at her noble feet for dinner.

Chas: The noble lady asks for my body yet, to be present in her apartment?

Mess: She does, sir. As though it were your apartment, sir.

18

Chas:	Tell me, man . . .
Mess:	Yes, sir?
Chas:	Do I look all right? Are my pants creased properly? Are my dungaroos falling out? I cant see in the back. . .
Mess:	It's such an unfortunate fall that you have come to ask me this after many years of my unhumble servitude. . . your ties are atrocious, sir.
Chas:	Oh, my boy, what, what, do you actually--tell me, are you in close acquaintance with this lady?
Mess:	Oh indeed! We've seen many a haystack in the lime of our life-light.
Chas:	Oh, my man, youre more than a servant. Tell me, do you think she will like blue?
Mess:	Methinks it goes not well with red my lord, and as she sees yon Phillip's hand in bloody shield, she too will want your redden cloak to put upon the outside of your bloody chest.
Chas:	*(confused)* Ah! Then soon my blue smoke will be toked and scattered to the wind, huh?
Mess:	You know it.
Chas:	It means slipping under sheets is more than twice above l'average level. . .
Mess:	I mean that the sheets you now must have go all the way over your head, my lord.
Chas:	Oh. . . Then off! And to the trough with you. Your face is ugly. *(both exit. Charles knocks at Ernestine's tent.)*
Ern:	Enter.
Chas:	My lady. You beckoned my call?
Ern:	I called your bet. Tell me Charles, must you wear those ugly blue ties? They go so lofty with the red I soon shall implant upon your torn out heart.
Chas:	Gladly I would cast them off dear lady if only you speak the word.
Ern:	My servant tells me of your shield in bloody hand, this same oft-uttered phrase which now impunes upon the very ridgements of battle. Have you Phillip's nose intact?

Chas: My lady, I have it even now in the saddlebag
        of yon hearse.

Ern: Certainly. Oh, youre some kind of wimp; you dont
        carry with you the shield upon which youve laid
        your body for the trip?

Chas: Oh, faith! of course, why, speak you of the shield?
        I thought you bespoke me of the nose, I have the
        shield right here in my tunic--

        (enter ghost of Phillip)

Ern: Stop sir stop! But what's that? Why it's some. . .
        it's floating above us.

Chas: Oh my goodness. . . I dont know. My lady, have you
        seen this premonition before?

Ern: Certainly. Every night in bed: It's *Phillip!*

Chas: Phillip!! Argh, I thought I slayed you once before in
        battle! I thought me lifted the sword from
        your burning body!

Phil: You cant slay me. Dont you know, Charles, I'm not
        but my self, my *ghost?*

Chas: *(wildly)* Nay. . . nay ghost. . . b . . .

Phil: Drop you your humble knife knave.

Chas: Phillip--I beseech thee--

Phil: Cut this watermelon for me.

Chas: Oh, Certainly. My lord, I beseech thee please
        to have mercy. I came upon you when you were
        already dud. I simply lifted the glorious metal
        from your bod.

Phil: Eat that watermelon, Charles, feel the venomous
        rush of the very wine you fed to me.

Chas: *(gagging)* Oh my God! He's given me the same wine?

Phil: No, the same water, melon. . .

Chas: Water? . . . I ask you, why do you haunt me?

Phil: Charles, youre such a good boy, but you know
        how I feel you.

Chas·   Oh. . . so, at last it's revealed to me. The secret
        torment which was beset me in my bed night after
        night, the great itching fingers crawling up my arse?

Phil: That is it, Charles. Soon you shall die of the
        ruby-red with the seedy, and you shall join me in
        blissful beddy-bye--to the end. . . the very end, Charles.

20

Chas: (*rallying*) You always snorted too much. An I saw you
          erelong from afar, I knew that I must get your goat.
          And so I approached you on the battle front, but font!
          you had already slipped under the mighty goad of the
          primping snare. And I, lying beside you, felt no breath
          enter from your nostrils. I picked up your shield, I cut
          off your nose, dear nose, and I slipped it into my pocket--
          er, saddlebag, and hence to this fine lady's offices. And
          I want you to know, Phillip, that I meant thee no harm.
          Please, do not give me the sheets that have been promised
          me. I want to live longer. I want to cast off this tunic
          and this blue tie which has been everforth repented for
          me. Dont you see, Phillip? Long hard years have I to
          live, and still you want to cut me off? I'll not let thee!
          Ah! be thee ghost or no ghost, I'll rip thee asunder!
          (*a clash of steel and Charles gulps*)

Phil: My God!

Chas: I'm ripped asunder myself. Lady, why did you not
          forewarn me of that razor blade lying on your table?

Ern: Charles, my only blood is with Phillip.

Chas: I feel that my blood is leaving and issues from Phillip's
          snorting nose. Ernestine, did you take me in?

Ern: Yes, some of my blood is transvite.

Chas: This slit will not be sewed up soon. I've got to go out
          on my own home ground to die quietly. Oh, can I
          make it? Lady. . . carry my in a bowl. . .
          (*he exits, crawling*)

Ern: Charles, what have I done? I have caused thee a rent
          to be paid too soon, brought you to a crawl upon your
          knees across the 3-mile desert. My designing has
          brought me no fast fabric of peaceful duplicity. Even
          you, Phillip, are nothing left but a spirit of the king
          who once sparkled through his halls. My tunnel has
          fallen in on me. Even my Turks doubt me. Phillip,
          I have failed and my reason falters. . .

Phil: Ernestive, Ernestine, though you have betrayed me,
          have sold me into Egypt; even though the camels
          now wait upon me; even though they have no witness
          but the halter by which I lead them; even still, it's
          you I love, Ernestine, I would have given you all the

armies and leggins you wanted. I'd have stripped
my son of his rank honor and vested you with my
good nose. You were everything to me and the
servants and rats and even Charles I forgave you
but now I'm dead and my kingdom without a
head needs you to guide my brainless son. Go
back and lead my land fill well you know you must
and I'll be watching there and waiting, till you come
to join me in that great bar where the little children
are not allowed. . . *(ghost exits, floating)*

Ern: Phillip, you once sat so heavy on your bedded
throne; now youre thinner than soup; youre misty in
my eyes. I never missed you but now I am missing in
battle what was the cause of my commotion. I looked
for my promotion ad hoc, I shopped around; but I
only wanted to cook for you, I think. I dont know.
I'll drown in a draught. Who cares? Only my son the
meaningless one. I fear for the country. Commercial
causes will overcome us. Hear them gurgle? No more
featherless clucks. I'll stick to my turkeys. I'll head
a feathery kingdom, a feather head!
(she/he collapses. baroque music.)

A. J. K.:   And thus ends episode 6, the turning chapter in
the final circle, the turntable account. Watch next
time for episode 7, when we will be witnessing
the explosion of the vast family tree, and the several
diggings-out of Phillip, the deceased king's, artificial
holdings. This is A.J.K. Waterbottomly--goodnight.

END

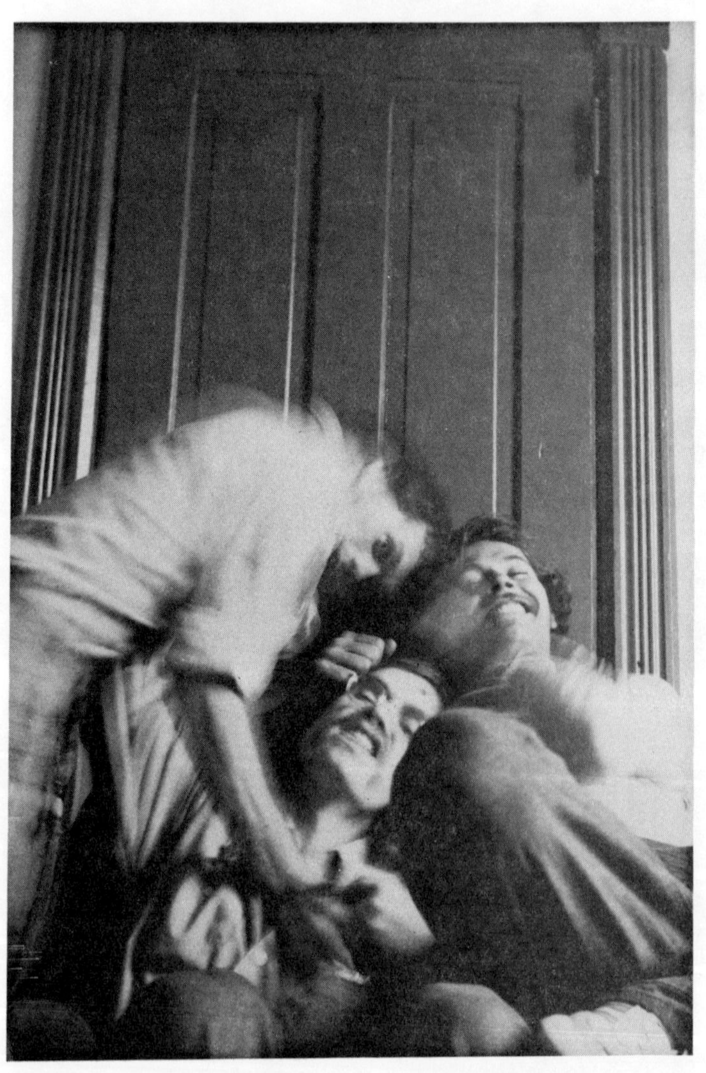

I DONT WANT THE RICE TO KNOCK ME DOWN

an abstraction

'Nowhere is the place to be.'
Spitshine Boots

g: We alternately hit and hug.

n: Glancing sideways from day to day our eyes melt together

g: in a common space somewhere between. Weather grows,

c: climate builds in piles of thunder speaking across
the short sky!

g: Small birds make it easily from side to side.

all: We pass across each other cloudy sun over cloudy sun
our magnetic bodies storm and dry for 4 or 5 years
we have bubbled our twin volcano heads down into
this valley!

n: When will it fill up?

g: Time opens all wounds.

n: Yeah, and speaking of colors, just listen to this:

> moon light grey the spectre shadowed his body
> emptied his pockets of reasoning direction
> > i groan in my knowledge heaped rubbish
> > i am in the rain i dont enjoy it
>
> the rain scattered his vision
>
> biting through his muscles that tied him
> he flew, sprang into space, swallowed himself
> > as i swallow the sky i swallow myself
> > under the sun i melt but i eat it
> > i speak colors i hear movement
> > i already escape the trap which drew me
> > out of my real bloodstream
>
> as he fell he rose
> control was not necessary
> > see where i am what i have
> > i give it to you all
> he had expanded to all extremes
> what was left was him as well

he knew it was raining on his mountains
he broke through the clouds riding sunlight
the wind rose in his throat, he sang,
he sang

Piece together this poem, piece together this poem,
piece together, piece, peace, Peace, PEACE!
(g knocks n down)
Know what I'd like to be? A square.

c: Easier than a circle. Your arm wont bend that way.

n: No I wont bend that way but over backwards fr yew
dear, fr yew dear I'd spill the beans fr yew dear,
fr yew dear I'd spill the coffee beans. . .

g: Where is she with our coffee? By god if this restaurant
isnt sinking I'll eat it.

n: See, the only way you can get a full cup is if you own the
place.

c: Art sake! The comic consciousness reduced to a mess hall!

n: And you cant do that without the Great Steamy.

all: *(chanting)* O Great Steamy, you make the black crude bubbly
out our lips, drooly along a conveyor of conversation belting
out our demands and making the righteous tremble for the
want of tips which we and not they do get for nothing. Yea,
those righteous neglect us and your manifestation on and on
forever.

c: And that's who we're all waiting for. You see doc, I need
stimulation. . . I need caffein. . . I need coffee. . . I . . .
(he falls)

n: He's down. Hang up and dial again.

c: I need attention immediately.

all: *(in rising panic)* Sure do like coffee. . . sure would like
some coffee. . . I. . . I'm getting shaky. . . coffee. . . we've
got to have coffee here. . . coffee!

g: Get off! Remember reward-and-punishment.

n: O yes, take your punishment and then get your reward.
Let's see, what was first?

g: 'You shall let no goblins in your forehead.'

c: Yeah, you shall make no kickbacks on your god.

n: You shall not sub-let your apartment.

g: Ya got to take the Lord serious, son. When yr
      standin before Him ya cant be gigglin.

n: How do you know?

g: I saw the lord, standin on the rooftop.

all: Yeah? Yeah?

g: I saw the lord, standin on the rooftop!

all: Yeah? Yeah?

g: I saw the lord, standin on the rooftop!

all: Yeah! Yeah!

g: Wearin a white nightgown! O baby. . .

all: *(singing)*

        I saw the lord standin on the rooftop
        I saw the lord standin on the rooftop
        I saw the lord standin on the rooftop
        Wearin a white nightgown.   O baby

        Went to the church lookin for salvation
        (Yeah, yeah, standin on the rooftop)

        Couldnt get in without an invitation
        (Yeah, yeah, stranded on the rooftop)

        Looked in my suit coat, saw the lord awaitin
        That's where he's always been.   O baby

        I saw the lord standin on the rooftop
        I saw the lord standin on the rooftop
        I saw the lord standin on the rooftop
        Wearin a white nightgown!

c: And Jabe stood before the altar, calling to the lord.

g: Lord, Lord. Lord. Lord? Lord lord? Lord! Lord lord lord!
      (he is struck by lightning)
      Got to look like a saint. It's all in the presentation.
      I need a sackcloth.

n: I'm sorry sir, this is the martyrs' section.
      Please present your credentials to the receptionist.

g: The receptionist? O my head. . . *(he wanders off)*

n: He's so confused.

c: But with god it's all men in order of their class.

n: Yes, and upstaging just cant go unchecked.

c: Besides, one never smiles into the face of god.

g: *(entering)* I'm afraid I've left my credentials, sir.

n: Hmmmm. I'm afraid we'll need some further proof.
      (begins to beat him with every sentence.)
      The lord pounds his rhythm out. His servants witness
      his power. Forever. Amen.

g: Lord, lord. . .

c: And Jabe gave himself to the angel to be tested as a martyr.

g: Druthers and cistern, revvin' Ack has given us a story to make
      us think. Jabe gave himself to the lord, to be kicked and
      shit on--er, spit on-- because he knew: he hadnt no other
      choice. We're in the same rowboat, friends, with the great
      paddler himself.

n: Yes, and pastor Bacco said that only the right wing and
      those who practice conserve will be saved.

g: Yea! For the lord paddles his boat with but one oar.

c: And no one can serve part time but must give it all
      and his money for that cause he would effect.

g: The river of the lord has one current: A. C.
      Acceptable Credentials! We must float his raft or sink. . .

n: And as a god in training I must shield myself from the unclean
      and build up my stores on earth and take all that you good
      people out of the goodness of your hearts and the thickness
      of your pocketbooks, will put into this little pastor-baggie
      that revvin' Ack is passing around right now.

c: And if you think you can serve the lord without them, yr
      dreamin. . . yr dreamin. . . you're dreaming again Mr.
      Phillips. Now why isnt that contract drawn up, those papers
      typed up, those restrooms cleaned up, that sawdust swept
      up? *(beats him severely.)* Have a nice weekend.

g: Thank you.

c: Yes, these are the cotton fields of today--the slow, weed-
      filled rows of American hired hands itching for their
      paychecks, cursing through the veins of people like me,
      money getherers, our hot blood rivers as wide as the
      Mississippi, as swift as the Columbia, broken bottles and
      derelicts of old labor leaders strewing our beaches and
      floating along from weekend to settlement-ridden weekend.
      Yet who appreciates us? Not the secretaries, typing the
      memos and swiveling from side to side. Not the janitors,
      who cant wait for us to leave so they can start rifling our
      desks. No, no one appreciates us executives. O me, we
      work so hard, boohoo, nobody cares, ohhhhh. . .

g: The blade is dull, it wanders wearily from garbage pile
      to garbage pile. Too much wax.

c: We press and offset press, the economy waxes strong.

n: Shine on hardest moon up in the sky. Grind on,
      grind on hardest moon, for me and my pail.

g: And yet soon it darks,

c: the street light blades out with the business punch,

n: angry children, left sightless,

c: covered by those waxen hands,

n: feel their way along a slippery surface to their
      little beddies by the heaps of detached paycheck stubs.

c: How do you know?

g: I am the book they open out of the closet where they mare
      at night, why should I clue you in when any street corner
      news stand could be as much a home as a pile of detached
      paycheck stubs.

all: It's better to be a working jerk
            and sit on your stubs,
            Aid all men with money
            a tower they do above us.

g: Yeah, the taste of that fresh cabbage, more important than
      the taste of. . .

n: Yes, he is a truly fine man. His friends and associates
      referred to him as. . .

c: More pleasant than the taste of . . .

g: The respectful silence warmed with its arms over her
      she sank drowsily like a ship below the surface of the
      plane she imagined the high arms of her chair formed. . .

c: And into it I could pour all my art and get none back but
      one teaspoonfull. And what about the really good taste of. .

n: She collapsed into a dream.

g: Yeah man, a really good dream.

n: Yeah man, very excellent.

c: Yeah man, one a da best.

all: Yeah man, one a da most important dreams of my life
      ah ha ha ha. . . *(they scuffle and box each other.)*

g: Wait a minute. Look, I can see you're really up for this
      but I'm not. Couldnt we just pretend we never saw each
      other and let it go?

n: Let it go. I see. I told you the first day we met never to let
      go because white collar jobs just dont have enough pull.

c: and then there's Semi-Insured Risks and Fractured Junkets,
      and Mutually Improvable Assets and complex ways of
      thinking you've never even heard of.

g: I dont get it.

n: You dont need it.

g: No really. One minute my mother is pulling me up out of
      the mud and the next I'm diving into a pay pool so thick
      there's no air at all below two feet.

c: You cant see anything, you cant feel anything,
      what a place to be. You're in an aquarium.

n: I dont see how people can expect you to breathe
      the same air they do. What are you doing?

g: Rolling down the red carpet.

c: Apparently the events of his life have left him nowhere.

n: *(singing)* Nowhere is the place to be, nowhere it is the
      place to be. . .

g: O no man you got it all wrong. Country and western is
      where it's at today. Just listen to this.

n: *(singing)*
                    You've been living a hard line
                    and I've got to say it shows,
                    there's a callous on your shouler
                    from holding them doorways closed.

                    But yr starting to get older,
                    yr strength is beginning to wane.
                    Come back, come back from nowhere,
                    and back into somewhere again.

all: *(chorus)*
                    He said nowhere yes nowhere's the place to be,
                    come all, come all,
                    nowhere yes nowhere's the place to be,
                    come all come with me.

n: But he would not listen,
                    he would not hear what I said.
                    We found him two days later,
                    by then of course he was dead.

        Now the doctor said he died
        of cancer of the shoulder.
        But we all know he died
        from living to long in nowhere.

all: He said nowhere yes nowhere's the place to be,
         come all, come all,
         nowhere yes nowhere's the place to be,
         come all come all with me.

g: Y'know, coming back from nowhere like we just did is
         one of the best ways to release your homespun tensions
         and get greater speed for your speaking dollar.

n: That's absolutely right Kipe--say, can I return again later?

c: Start when you're young and go until you drop over.
         That's the only way to tell for sure.

g: And speaking of surety, let's drop over to the other side of
         the coin and see who's falling out down there. Bill?

n: Thank you Ted for allowing me these few moments to wrap
         up my feelings about this great sight. The green chill in the
         air, the surge of the wind over the crest of the huge silver
         statue descending out of the sky, all bring me to the edge
         of reality to stand yawning over the great preposition.

g: Have you seen any sureties, Bill?

n: I'm waiting to find that out now. Take five.

c: Is that what we follow our to meal for meal for to wait?

g: No, but a silver fog'll get you two tanks of gas for a free
         meal to shoes. --fter that brief wait-down coverage
         interruption, we return you to. . . the sinking ship.

n: Delicate little fishes were run down today by the Queen
         Bailey in an offshore incident which Human Society
         officials called 'no decent way to begin peacemaking
         ventures with our precious oceans.' More barney than
         barnacle perhaps, but with the recent trend toward
         animalism we cant be too careful.

c: Recent animated uprisings in fringe coat dress areas
         and east coasts have been triggered by the Freedom Day
         festivities brought on by the recent annexation of
         Massachusetts by Britain. Nobody doubts that this
         is the most disgusting displace of arrogance since
         Charlie bit Pico in the seventh.

all: *(speaking simultaneously in collage)*
. . . Bill Ding took his life in his hands today and
jumped from the roof of his job but. . .
. . . the bomb was said to have exploded when the
senator opened his suitcoat. . .
. . . Johnny Comebarely, vice president and spokesperson
for the corporation. . .
. . . said that panic first cropped up in a poorly
insinuated attic. . .
. . . that px officials were in no way trying to
regulate the flow of bayonets. . .
. . . said to have this happen now is just the worst
possible thing that could have happened. . .

n: And you cant get it back, and they cant. No time to
re-rent the party! And I cant think of a better life than
that!

g: O yes you can. With my money back technique you can
make up to 50 pots of coffee per day, with no or little
cleanup. Put me in your house and let me fill the room.
With the aroma of dark. . .
hot. . .   steamy. . .

all: We pass across each other cloudy sun over cloudy
sun the mouths of our minds open and howling
mixing out rounds and rolling our own oats. . .
I ate such a big meal. It was great!

n: And I can tell you, that the grass is green and
anything tastes good with the proper season.

c: In the name of Jesus Christ, amen.

END

THE DEFENDANT

a grammar trial

characters:

the **Judge**
Mr. People, the prosecutor
Mr. Utah, the defense attorney
Barn Cleetley, witness
Mr. Crosby, defendant
Bailiff
Clerk

setting:

A Courtroom. The Judge and the two attorneys apparently regard their jobs with humor. They speak casually throughout the trial, pretending to be competent.

scene 1

Bailiff: All rise! *(shuffling. Mr. Utah and Mr. People whisper together.)* Be seated.

Judge: Case No. 671, the People vs. . .

Mr. People: Crosby.

Judge: Crosby. *(gavel)* Is the prosecutor ready to begin the questioning?

Mr. People: Yes, your honor, we have been prepared to make some opening remarks when it fits your leisure, sir.

Judge: Please, please begin.

Mr. People: *(dramatically)* In this case, we are not merely talking about grammar in a high and aloof sense that most of us have come up to know it as being. We are rather hoping to. . . to prove to you that the flatness and longevity that language has come to know now, can be expanded to include a fuller bustline, more peanuts per bag, and the revolving penny. So, keep these things in your heart as we will present our case.

Judge: Thank you. Does the defense wish to make any opening remarks?

Mr. Utah: The defense, for its rebuttal, will merely state that it
is our contention--and we feel it is a true and consti-
tutional contention--that the State has overstepped--
and not for the first time perhaps--we have decided
to make this a test case. Because we often find the
State out of its grammatical bag and into what is
properly speaking, the people's own business--that
is to say, or minding; and--

Judge: The time of the speaker has expired. Would the
prosecution please call your first witness?

Mr. People: Your honor, as our first witness we would like to call
Barn Cleetley, who is a professor at Mit University and
has written several books on the subject of erroneous
grammar.

Bailiff: Barn Cleetley to the stand. Raise you right hand. Do
you swear that what you tell this court shall be the
whole truth and nothing but the truth so help you God?

Cleetley: Do I have to?

Bailiff: If you're going to witness for this court, yes.

Cleetley: I didnt want to witness for this court.

Mr. People: He is considered a hostile witness, your honor. We
intend to lead him around this courtroom.

Judge: Take your stand, son.

Mr. People: Now then, Mr. Cleetley--*Dr.* Cleetley. How many
years have you been a grammarian?

Cleetley: *(gruffly)* Sixty.

Mr. People: Are you a naturalized citizen?

Cleetley: *(contemptuously)* Of course. Who could speak english
without a permit?

Mr. People: Do you have a family?

Cleetley: I have. . . I have a wife.

Mr. Utah: Defense objects.

Judge: On what grounds?

Mr. Utah: This is misleading questioning. Impertinencies.

Judge: Mr. Utah, I must overrule that objection.
Please proceed, Mr. People.

Mr. People: *(rocking in a rocking chair)* Now then, Mr. Cleet--
Dr. Cleetley. When you were first introduced to the
statement made by the defendant--

Judge: Just a minute! I never heard of a prosecuting attorney
sitting in a rocking chair. I dont feel that I'm **required**
to spend my time in the presence of such indignities--

Mr. People: Pardon me, your honor. I'll move to the bench. . .
Your honor, uh, you seem to be destroying my train
of thought.

Judge: I'm not your honor.

Mr. People: You're my son. Please, go on. Now, Mr. Cleetley--

Judge: Please, Mr. Prosecutor. . .

Mr. Utah: Objection!

Judge: On what grounds?

Mr. Utah: Nepotism. Incest.

Mr. People: Overruled.

Judge: *(exasperated)* The gentlemen would please approach
the bench. *(they approach)*

Mr. People: Yes, your honor?

Judge: I feel that there is some necessity that we should
prolong this matter until after the first break; therefore,
I'm going to suggest a recess. What do you say to this?

Mr. Utah: I'll accept that.

Judge: I'll meet you out by the jungle gym.

Bailiff: All rise.

Judge: The court will recess until 2 o'clock this afternoon.

Bailiff: Now--at the sound of the tone: Beep!
(shuffling of people leaving courtroom)

Mr. Utah: This is going to be one of the slowest trials. . .

Mr. People: I dont know. I cant think at all lately. . .

scene 2

Judge: *(enters talking to Mr. Utah and Mr. People)*
--this case is as strong as ever. Ahem. *(gavel)*
Would the defendant please rise. You have been
charged with colloquialism in the incident of the
speech of May 31, 1971. What, do you have any,
uh how do you wish to plead?

Mr. Utah: Not guilty.

Judge: Not guilty. Yes, of course. Heh-heh.

Mr. People: Your honor, there is a second count of vagary.

Judge: Oh, vagary. I thought that was a misprint.
Uh, yes, vagary. Well, would the prosecution please
call the first witness.

Mr. People: Didnt we call the first witness, your honor?

Judge: Well, I dont seem to recall, but uh. . .

Mr. People: Mr. Cleetley.

Mr. Utah: *Dr.* Cleetley.

Mr. People: *Dr.* Cleetley.

Judge: Oh yes, Dr. Cleetley.

Mr. Utah: We left him on the stand.

Mr. People: I would like to recall Dr. Cleetley and resume the prosecution at this high level of strategic comment.

Bailiff: Dr. Cleetley to the stand!

Cleetley: *(approaching, disgruntled)* How many times. . . *(he sits.)*

Mr. People: Dr. Cleetley. In your experience as a grammarian and within the confines of the State you are sworn to uphold and the laws pertaining to that State, what would be your expert opinion as to the statement, 'When the going get toughs, the toughs get going.'?

Cleetley: *(carefully)* I find the statement to be interesting, grammatically speaking. I dont pretend to be a linguist; I'm an accountant for Cecil, Burns and Fillmore and uh--

Mr. People: Dr. Cleetley! You said you'd been a grammarian for 60 years!

Cleetley: I'm a grammarian; of course I'm a grammarian, but I'm not a linguist and this is a charge of colloquialism, · and I just dont feel that I'm qualified to rule on this issue, but I'd be glad to give you my personal opinion--

Mr. Utah: Objection! The witness must answer the question.

Cleetley: Would you repeat that?

Mr. People: Would the witness please answer the question?

Cleetley: Oh. . . I feel that it's possible, yes.

Mr. People: Thank you, Dr. Cleetley. Now, as a grammarian, could you tell us something about the origin of the word 'toughs'?

Cleetley: 'Toughs' was first introduced into the english language in the fourteenth century where it was used to denote goose eggs and chicken brawls. This gradually, through a sequence of transitory progressions which crossed the English Channel at least 12 times and ruled out all possibility of negligent--

Mr. People: Thank you, Doctor.

Cleetley: --release of--but there's more--

Mr. People: I'm sure that's sufficient for the jury.

Cleetley: --you see, up until the nineteenth century there was--

Mr. People: Could you tell us something--

Cleetley: But there was a time when--

Mr. People: Your honor!. . . *(They go on talking over each other
              until the Judge gavels angrily.)*

Judge: Order! *(They stop talking abruptly)* If there is another
              disturbance like this I shall be cleared the court!

Mr. People: Now then Mr. Cleetley--

Mr. Utah: The defense would like to rule for a mistrial.

Mr. People: On what grounds?

Judge: *(impatiently)* Objection overruled! Now please go
              on with the questioning.

Mr. People: Yes. *(to Cleetley)* Is there not a medieval ladle which
              was often referred to as a 'going' and uh, could it not
              be this word in which the defendant context himself
              at the moment of this statement?

Cleetley: It could be, except for one simple and, I might add,
              rather obvious detail; and that is the word 'gets'.
              (He hisses the 's' several times.)

Mr. People: Ah ha, but you see, 'toughs' are supposed to be
              chickens, are they not? Chicken brawls.

Cleetley: Chicken brawls or turkey eggs, like I said.

Mr. People: Uh, yes, and, what do you dip chicken with but a
              ladle? Ah ha! Now--

Cleetley: But the goings dont 'gets' tough! 'Goings' is plural
              and 'gets' is singular. For this reason I have decided
              that that particular avenue of research is out of order.
              Now, you're calling me as an expert witness; dont
              you want to accept my opinion on this matter at all?

Mr. People: That will be all, Mr. Cleetley.

Cleetley: *(speaking louder)* I feel that I've been in the opinion-
              ating business for 12 years and I've given myself over--

Mr. People: Dr. Cleetley. . .

Cleetley: --when nothing else could defend them but the
              grammar--

Mr. People: Would the defense take the witness out, please?

Mr. Utah: The defense wishes to cross-examine the witness.

Judge: Very well, proceed.

Mr. Utah: Dr. Cleetley. Is it true that you were once pungent?

Cleetley: Who's on trial here?

Mr. Utah: No, bear with this line of questioning. I would like to expose to the judge and the jury and the G. P. that this witness, masquerading as a grammarian of reknown is as he said a mere stock holder, stock broker, and stock taker. *(Mr. Cleetley grumbles.)* So then, I will carry on. If you allege that 'going' is singular and 'gets' is plural, what are 'toughs'?

Cleetley: 'Toughs' is obviously plural. What are you, some kind of idiot?

Mr. Utah: Well, why, if 'toughs' is plural and 'going' is plural--

Mr. People &
Mr. Utah: *(in unison)* --Why should 'gets' be plural?

Cleetley: Dont you remember the anti-segregation ruling of 1612? My god, you're a lawyer, you ought to know these things.

Mr. Utah: Well, uh, disregarding Dr. Cleetley, or whoever this doctor, or so-called doctor, Doctor! Speaking of that, where uh, *(he laughs)* might we inquire the source of your credentials? Is it true you're a graduate of the University of Bologna in northern Italy?

Cleetley: Well. . .

Mr. Utah: Is it true or not true?

Cleetley: You have my record before you, you've played it several times in my own company and you said you liked my song very much. Now when are you going to give me a chance to prove myself on the air, . . . Mr. Barney. . . I . . . cant seem to recall. . .

Mr. Utah: *(interceding)* It must be amply clear to the jury and the judge that the testimony of this witness is not worth a farthing.

Cleetley: I'm--I'm conscious, but I'm confused. . .

Mr. People: Your honor, we're through with this witness; could you have him step out?

Judge: The witness will please step off. *(Cleetley exits noisily.)* Well, is the defense ready to present its case?

Mr. Utah: Yes; Mr. Crosby, the famous, will take the stand please.

Mr. People: Is there a comma after that name?

Bailiff: Mr. Comma Crosby please take the stand! Raise your
right hand. Do you swear that what you tell this
court shall be the truth and nothing but the truth
so help your god?

Crosby: I. . . uh. . . I . . . I . . . uh. . .

Mr. Utah: He will, your honor, no question about it. Uh. . .
your witness.

Mr. People: *(amused)* Well, since the defense has no defense, I
think we'll rest our case right here and leave it up to
the judge to decide who has presented their case here
today.

Judge: *(anxiously)* Now what happened to what you told me
in the lunch hour about you having him wrapped up
around your finger? Arent you going to present something that's going to give this crowd a thrill for this
trial? We havent seen anything yet, and by god as a
judge--

Mr. People: I'd like to point out that the other courtroom is
showing 'Ben Hur' and is getting more viewing audience than we are! Now we need some excitement in
this courtroom--

Judge: Procedure has been tainted here, and I want order,
I want peace, I want quiet--thank you. Now I want
you to go on with this defense as if you had some
kind of plan.

Mr. Utah: Yes, your honor. Mr. Crosby, have you ever heard
the phrase 'extremism in defense of liberty is no vice'?
Are you familiar with this phrase?

Crosby: I believe so, yes.

Mr. Utah: I see--

Mr. People: Objection, your honor. The defense is using colloquialism in its defense of colloquialism! I cant see this
in the legal rules at all.

Judge: Mr. People, I'm going to see this one out if you dont
mind.

Mr. Utah: Thank you, Judge. Quite au contraire; Why I am
employing these other quote or so-called colloquialisms
is that I would like to point out to the witness, the
defense and the jury, the utter prevalence of this type

41

of political remark in our life. For instance, the immortal former president Mr. Nixon's 'I am not a crook.' It is possible when he says this to be meaning something other than what he really says, dont you think so, Mr. Crosby?

Mr. People: Objection, your honor, the defense is employing vagary.

Judge: I'll withhold--I'll uphold that objection, Mr. People. *(to Mr. Utah)* Please keep your remarks to the matter at hand.

Mr. Utah: All right.

Judge: By the way, Mr. Utah, you may not have noticed but we have a witness on the stand.

Mr. Utah: I thought I was examining him. He's my witness.

Judge: I thought you were speaking rhetorically. I thought you had lapsed into a Senate recall debate pattern.

Mr. Utah: The reason I brought this candidate, or excuse me, he is no candidate, forget that. *(all laugh.)*

Judge: He's a candidate for jail, Mr. Utah.

Crosby: Doesnt anybody believe in me?

Mr. Utah: No, no. Mr. Crosby took the stand not so much with the feeling that he had to defend himself; of course you know under our system of law you neednt defend yourself. He took the stand because he felt he had a plus in this case, and he was going to hang it over the edge of Mr. People and the prosecutor's cross-exam- ination--

Crosby: Can I tell them now?

Mr. Utah: --and so I have no further points to make; merely that no matter how old language gets--

Crosby: Ask me the question!

Mr. Utah: --the possibility of it being colloquial--

Crosby: *(urgently)* The question!

Mr. People: Your honor, your honor, objection! The witness is coaching his counsellor.

Judge: I agree; that's true. You will please remain quiet until you are asked a question. I dont care if you are on the witness stand, you wont speak out of turn!

Mr. Utah: Thank you, your honor.

Mr. People: Would the defense counsel please get on with the questioning?

Mr. Utah: The defense counsel would like to make one last question. You're accused of vagary and colloquialism. Do you have any idea what that is?

Crosby: Well, yes. I learned about it once.

Mr. Utah: And you're innocent of these charges, are you not?

Crosby: Well, sure; you said you'd do it for me. . .

Mr. Utah: Have you ever willingly colloquialised, or vaged?

Crosby: Well. . .

Judge: Mr. Utah, I've got to make a bench objection at this point. Your use of the rules of grammar is very slip-shod indeed. You forget that it doesnt matter if the accused or any other private citizen uses colloquialism or vagary or any other private pleasure in his home or office; it's only in the matter of public forum and debate that this issue becomes one of national devolvement. So, on that point please reword your question.

Mr. Utah: My question, ever so slightly reworded, was that. . . had you ever employed language in such a way as to colloquialise the listener and cause them to have feelings of homeyness, rather than thoughts that we could use in the public debate. In other words, were you appealing to their gross emotions, or were you appealing to their better intellect? That seems to me to be the final criterion for language.

Crosby: I--I dont know what to say. I'm--I'm confused. You said you'd ask me a question and, I've forgotten. What was the question?

Mr. Utah: The question is, are you innocent or guilty?

Crosby: I'm uh. . . well, I'm . . . uh. . . your honor, may I make a statement?

Mr. Utah: Your honor, your honor. . .

Mr. People: Your honor, I--

Mr. Utah: Mr. People, may I speak a private moment with the witness?

Mr. People: Of course.

Mr. Utah: *(whispering to Crosby)* You realize, that if you commit guilty to this charge you're going up the river and neither of us will ever see the outside of this courtroom again. So you've got to tighten up.

Crosby: I know, but what am I going to do about the--I cant say that I didnt say it, and I cant say that I have any respect for the People, so what am I going to give him with all these people watching?

Mr. Utah: When the prosecutor asks you if you said it, admit you said it, but point out how good you are in your heart.

Crosby: Oh yeah, right, the good heart speech. I remember.

Mr. Utah: Yeah, yeah.

Crosby: Well, I'm just so nervous. You've got to ask me the questions that I--

Mr. People: Your honor, can we get on with this? The witness has had his time out period.

Mr. Utah: All right, all right. Thank you your honor. Your witness. Prosecution's witness.

Mr. People: Mr. . . uh. . . what's the name?

Mr. Utah: Crosby.

Mr. People: Crosby. It is true, is it not, that on the evening of September 24, 1971 you did make a speech in which you pointed out, or used the sentence, 'When the toughs get going, the goings get toughs.' Did you not?

Crosby: I believe the wording was '. . .the goings gets toughs.'

Mr. Utah: Objection!

Judge: Yes Mr. Utah?

Mr. Utah: We've been distorted out of the real.

Judge: I beg your pardon?

Mr. Utah: The phrase, for the court; would you read in the court record what the actual phrase was? Would the clerk please read that?

Clerk: 'When the toughs get going, the going' --excuse me, your honor. 'When the goings'--*(he giggles.)* 'When the'-- *(The entire court breaks into hysterical laughter, except Crosby. The clerk tries to control himself.)* 'When the goings gets toughs, the toughs gets goings.'

Mr. People: *(still laughing)* Thank you, thank you, clerk. *(He collects himself.)* Now then. You did make this speech. We have heard expert testimony in this trial today that 'toughs' and 'goings' are colloquial terms first branded in the fourteenth century by Liz-- Lizabeth IV in her stable at Rhinesburger. Now. can you say that you, a man who once graduated from Mit University, a loyal and dependable hardhat from upper Michigan, were not aware of these colloquial terms, in the context of our well-read and certainly brilliant society today? Could you answer me straight on that, sir?

Crosby: *(dodging)* I've read Mezvinsky's *Twelve Disciples,* I've read the *Trash of Mongul Heap,* and I am aware that there are mystical proportions that require traitorous action on the part of the believer, and I dont believe in those. I dont believe in them. I spoke out of pure humbleness to the capacity of my constituents to absorb anything I could give them--

Mr. People: Excuse me, Mr. Crosby. Could you explain to me what the word 'daeji' means?

Mr. Utah: Objection.

Crosby: Yes, indeed.

Judge: Mr. Utah?

Mr. Utah: Uh, overruled. I'd like to know what that word means.

Crosby: 'Daeji' is a colloquialism which refers to a certain dialectual grouping of German east smatterings. I dont personally use those kind of words, you understand.

Mr. People: Ah, but you are familiar with them?

Crosby: Well, I've heard them around the office. The President used to mention 'daisies' and 'dags'--

Mr. People: Mr. Crosby, what is a 'kip'?

Crosby: A 'kip' in White House jargon means a dive, or a take--

Mr. People: Would you consider that to be a colloquial word?

Crosby: --in other words, as per the transcripts, Mr. Ehrbob spoke of Mr. Hacko as being "on the kip".

Mr. People: Thank you. Now, we have seen that words which you yourself, you say, do not use; words that I'm sure many of the courtroom audience and technicians dont know; and those of us who only watch t.v. dont hear--

Crosby: It doesnt matter if they know them or not. It's simply
            a matter of it the President said them.

Mr. People: But you cannot deny, sir, that if you know
            these words you certainly must be aware of the
            colloquial origins of 'toughs' and 'goings', and it
            must indeed show upon the record and upon your
            face, smattered with German blood and all the
            rest, that you must have been aware--

Crosby: *(faltering)* I--I didnt say it because I was aware of
            anything, I--said it because--because, well. . . I told
            you why, because I was--

Mr. People: *(demanding)* Why did you say it, Mr. Crosby. Tell
            us why you said it!

Mr. Utah: Now, your honor, my witness is agitated. I move
            for a recess!

Mr. People: Tell us why you said it, Mr. Crosby!

Crosby: I--I wanted the votes. I wanted the votes.

Mr. Utah: *(alarmed)* I move for a recess!

Mr. People: The votes. You did it for the votes.

Crosby: Yes, I did it. *(overflowing)* In the great American
            Tradition. The time when all of us can be free
            enough to speak without laws and give ourselves up
            without haveing to be arrested. . .

Mr. People: Yes, ladies and gentlemen--

Mr. Utah: Remember the Alamo!

Mr. People: --another Senator so eager for Freedom Day--

Mr. Utah: 54--40 or fight!

Mr. People: --that his zealous jeal has overridden his better interest
            in the laws and the governing of the grammatical
            history of this country. An evil politician, ladies
            and gentlemen--

Judge: Order!

Mr. People: --a man not to be trusted with the pennies and
            babies that housewives now have given him. . .

Judge: Order! Order! . . .
            *(Mr. People continues to orate, Mr. Utah calls for
            mistrial, the Judge pounds his gavel, Mr. Crosby
            slumps in his chair, as the scene fades.)*

END

WALKING ON THE FEET OF THE FAITHFUL

a script for Radio

      (timpani drum roll)
g: If the impossible happend--so what?

      (fanfare)
n: It's the Voice of Idiocy Hour.

singers: O save me from
              the ancient hole
              and guide me to
              your sins again.

      (organ music)

g: A good book says (chapter 4 page 3):   "When the king knew the danger and saw it, he went to the people and cried his counsel and offered his arms; but the people rebelled, saying, 'We think you are stupid.' "

n: Incidentally, Gail, Today's good book is *I Draw The Lord* by Ernie Payday. But dont you think we can drive some message of interest to this generation's kings and poor people out of these words? You know, I'm always bumping into on the street--

g: --people who ask us, "What is the true way?" Well, we all know, it's the American Way. And you know, we talk with a lot of foreigners on this program, but today we're going to be interviewing some Americans about their faith and the springs it springs from. But first, here is my father H. R. Bishop with today's inspirational and confidential reading.

n: Today's words have been written for us by John Nutmeg of Coriander, Michigan. *(piano music; birds chirping)* I was 13 and I was walking along a road in our farming community, thinking about the wonders of nature as boys do, when to my immediate shock--I fell headlong down a well! Well, I was pretty shaken up. I stared into the blackness, upside down, and I felt it was all over. But then, right after I had almost given up, I remembered my dad talking about faith and I thought, now's the time to put faith to work. So I had faith

that the fire department would rescue me. I had faith
they would come in response to my yelling and shouting. And after about 20 minutes of faithfully scream-
ing and praying, the firemen came and lowered a rope
and pulled me out.

g: It sounds like Mr. Nutmeg discovered the power of faith
      at a very young age, dad.

n: Yes, it does say here that he was 13 at the time.

g: I'd like the people at home to know that we will be offering
      printed copies of today's program at the end. Now think
      about your own drastic changes as we listen to a song by
      Cynthia Promise titled, "I Know He's Coming Back".
      (Guitar fades up. sound of man singing)

n: He's run out on the country,
             He's run out on the sea,
             He tells us all we're eatin'
             But it just looks like chewin' to me.

all: *(chorus)*

             I know he's coming back to town,
             But when, it's hard to see,
             It's no use waiting for changes,
             The law's all that's left to me.

      (they hum the verse softly, gradually fading under:)

slim: So there I was, sprawled on the floor of that old shack deep
      in the Adirondacks, two of the most desperate criminals in
      the West staring down on my ruffled countenance...

tex: Yr kinda des'prate yrself, arent ya, Slim?

red: He's kinda criminal too, isn't he, Tex? Ha ha!

tex: Whadda *you* know?

red: I know as much as any of us critters about what's goin'
      on here in this cabin way off in the mountains...

slim: Red's right, Tex. What *does* any of us know of the destiny
      waitin' for us tonight, or tomorrow? But Red, I think yr
      exaggeratin' about this place bein' a cabin. It's more like
      a shack.

tex: Wal, I aint gonna shave myself about it tonight, boys. What
      ever it is, if it comes tonight, it'll find me sleepin'.

red: Yr about the galdurndest feller about sleepin', Hex.

tex: I oughta snake yr neck...

slim: Look boys, we may not get along too well; the three worst
      outlaws in three different states, holed up together; how
      could we? But just you think about what's out there
      waitin' and maybe you'll figure why we can respect each
      others gun hands. Y'know, in a way we get along very
      well.

tex: Say there, Rod, that pot's startin' to smell mighty good.
      What you cookin' up fr us?

red: It's a stew made from decalcified rhine-squirrels and
      mississippi trench-larvae.

tex: Yeah? Here, let's have a little look.
      *(sound of removing lid from stew pot, boiling; then
      amplified sound of insects rising to a peak and cutting
      off suddenly)*

red: What? What?

tex: Slim, why dont you get up off the floor?

slim: Ok, Tex.
      But I didnt get up. Not at first. I lay there on my back
      looking up at the roof. It began to look like the floor. I
      felt so much safer with Tex and Red, looking at them from
      a prone position. But why? Was it my eyes or was it the
      room that was spinning? Were my hands attached to my
      legs or not? O, that Indian sure knew his medicine--
      (Cut to discussion program)

prof: --but I dont really think he knows the meaning of style.

g: Why do you say that, Professor?

prof: I think you know why, Mr. Greg.

n: Maybe you should just explain it again in case any of our
      listeners isnt as aware of the realities as, uh, as we are.

prof: I mean simply that the President of the United States
      is not in a position to gamble with the integrity of the
      citizens. No one has positioned herself or himself into
      such a high level of strained sensibilities as has the
      President. To ask him take charge at this time would
      be futile. Yet someone must take charge when cities
      and countries are refusing with thanks to pay back their
      loans; give us the chance to spend our own money abroad!
      Nobody speaks like Americans, nobody speaks to them
      or for them but before them. Always, always, the
      President is selling America with a money back guarantee.
      Why not the other way around? Where is the grace, the

authority, where is the *faith?* Gimmick salesmanry, send U. S. flagpoles around the world, it's the pesky generation, dealing free, dealing freedom. . .

n: Maybe we should take a phone call . . .

g: That's a good idea. This is Ideas on the Move, hello what is your question?

slim
tex &

red: We'd like ta know what we're waitin' for up in these mountains.

g: Hello. You're on the air.

pres: This is the President of the United States. I'd like to ask the professor just what he means by integrity. . .
(fade up humming of "He's Run Out on the Country".)

g: --join with us in thanking you all from the bottom of Shortbreath Studios where the Choice of Idiots is produced each week. So until next time, this is Gale Hale saying, goodbye and--have a faithful week!
(Fade music.)

END

THE DOA SQUACK SHOW

a mixnmatch tv script

characters:

Chic Uttley,
Babyl Snurr, DOA host-journalists
Bonnie, studio technician
President of the United States Warborn
Gaylord Faerie, expert
Yamahaamahama Gohotli Yoga, yogi
Kid
Hardhat Father
Bill Daytona, famous ex-racer sports reporter

setting:

America, now. In the studios of DOA and on location.
These scenes may be arranged to taste.

News Opening

*(fadeup on news desk. There is a projection screen
behind. Babyl Snurr enters, turns on a switch by the
screen, walks to desk and turns on microphone.)*

Bab: This is the DOA television network newscasting from
the heart of America and always the most powerful
station in your area. Listen now as we wake you up
to the morning after.
*(relaxing music. Chic Uttley enters, they talk and
arrange news sheets and props. Then they go on
camera.)*
Hello, Chic, I hope to be seeing you again later as we
begin the morning.

Chic: I'm Chic Uttley and this is Babyl Snurr and this is the
DOA morning news instigation. Bab, did you get that
coffee?

Bab: I'm trying to get these directions straight; I thought
         I did what they told me but. . .
         (music fades.)

Chic: Here, try this can opener. Well, broadcasters, I hope
         you'll stay with us for the next 8 full hours of easy
         programming. We'll be here with news and up to date
         commentary on today's top billings, plus later on we'll
         be talking to a Mr. Crosby in connection with his
         alleged act of colloquialism.   Also Bab will have his
         report on Freedom Day and the reaction abroad.
         Right, Bab?

Bab: Right Chic, and of course we'll be presenting our
         overview of the collapse of the world--as we see it.
         But now. . . for those of you broadcasters who are
         tuning in for the first or last time, I remind you that
         everything we say is true. Our attention was brought
         up short by a prime example of that this morning when
         Chic Uttley's prediction that a major bounder by
         the British was ensuing, came true. Chic?

Chic: That's true, and it's today's top story, too. Last night
         in a robe which shocked the entire syllablized world,
         the Prime Minister of Great Britain, Quid Pound,
         announced that his country would annex Massachusetts.
         But don't get excited folks, because the date has been
         set for June 12, still several weeks away. A sleepy
         President Warborn stated that he will retaliate by
         proclaiming Freedom Day in the U. S. on June 12.
         Babyl, you have a comment, I think.

Bab: Thank you, Chic. In the wake-up of the storm, the
         President's main concern appeared to be for his
         electoral body. His 4-point plan would announce
         the suspending of all laws on June 12 in the form
         of Freedom Day, the uplifting of a spiritual ban on
         foreign tobacco products, relief for the survivors
         provided by the British government, and relieve the
         President of a nasty responsibility.

Chic: It just goes to show what can happen when nationalism
         gets carried away with itself. We fell pretty strongly
         about that here at DOA and we'll have more items in
         this vein later on, but now, in the lucky No. 1 spot,
         here is this morning's first commercial break-in.
         Roll tape one! *(blackout)*

Commercial

(fadeup)

Bab: Bonnie?

Bonnie: Yes. . . oh, yes? *(She is sitting on a vacant set eating crackers.)*

Bab: Bonnie, ever since you've been eating those crackers we havent been able to get a word out of you. Would you like a drink of water?

Bonnie: Yes, and I'm going to go get one right now, so we'll see you later, boys. *(exit)*

Bab: Bonnie doesnt know it but we've given her a cracker filled with salt. Now this salt is going to keep her thirsty no matter how much she drinks. Now let's just watch her and see how the fun goes.

Bonnie: *(entering)* Oh, I'm certainly glad you guys gave me that water. Say, can I have another cracker?

Bab: Bonnie, arent you thirsty? Here, have some more water.

Bonnie: Oh, thank you. *(She drinks.)*

Bab: *(to camera)* Bonnie is still drinking, she's gone through her second quart and she's, the judges--

Bonnie: Do you have any more water?

Bab: Oh yes, here's another quart. The judges are amazed that she even asked for another cracker after the first bottle. Uh, Bonnie?

Bonnie: *(gulping)* Wha--?

Bab: Would you like to tell the viewers how you like. . . uh, what you think about our crackers.

Bonnie: Well you know, uh, these crackers are wonderful. . . uh, wait a minute, I'm gonna go get some more water.

Bab: OK. *(to camera)* What Bonnie doesnt know is that the water we've given her is full of de-- uh, de-- what was that word?

Chic: *(off camera)* Desensitized!

Bab: Oh, desensitized salt, and this is going to keep her thirsty no matter how much water she drinks, so let's just watch as the fun continues to grow on this commercial message.

Bonnie: You know, I'm getting really sick of you guys putting water in my salt, now I want another cracker!

55

Bab: Bonnie, here's a cracker.

Bonnie: Gee thanks, Bab.

Bab: Just remember folks, people like Bonnie shouldnt be
around, and most of them arent, so crackers or no
crackers, we guarantee our product.
(blackout)

Feature

Chic: And now we switch you to our instant video playback
machine for an excerpt from the President's speech of
yesterday concerning Israel, the Middle East, and other,
uh, pertinent issues. Ladies and gentlemen, the
Resident of the United States.

President: Friends, I've come before you today, wanting to express
my views on why I have sent approximately one-half
million troops into Israel. I find, after grave consider-
ation, and much consultation with my cabinet members,
that to avoid any longer the issue in Israel would be to
avoid our duty as a world power. You know now that
approximately 55,000 American boys died in Vietnam.
I think it was a worthwhile gesture on my part to send
these boys over there, knowing as I did that many of
them would not return home. I feel however, that it
is the duty of the greatest country in the world to
protect those who are not able to protect themselves.
Therefore, I now make the following announcement.
Next week I will send approximately 65,000 American
troops into--Switzerland. I think that after reviewing
the situation brought on by the arrest of two Americans
in that country, you will be with me, and you will see
the necessity of such a move. I leave you now with one
message: remember that we *are* Americans, and as such
we want to put across the right image, to our friends
and our enemies abroad. Thank you very much.

Interview

Bab: Well all right. Early this morning as you may know,
broadcasters, an earthquake dropped Portugal 25
feet, and now with a DOA follow-up retort comm-
issioned just hours ago, I'd like to present a very fine
scientist who has developed something, a theory about
lines. So I'd like to introduce to you Mr. Gaylord
Faerie.

Gaylord: Well, it's --it's been my theory for several years that
uh lines. . . can think, and that they have a family
life uh, just as. . . humans do, and that they, they,
uh. . . well, you know, whatever families do. And uh,
mankind for several centuries has been very rude to
these lines, and you will see that lines are beginning
to go astray, because of this lack of guidance by
mankind. You will notice that there are more and
more, uh, crooked lines as you go along. These are
lines that have not had the right upbringing. Often
we call them cracks, but they're *lines,* and because
we call them cracks, this is offending them. Now,
I'd just like to say, I'm not trying to--to play prophet
or anything, but uh, ju--just as a little forecast, unless
we start treating these lines better, and giving them
their rights, and straightening them out, as you might
say, they're going to rise up against us. And so uh,
well anyway, that's all I have to say, I've done a lot
of work and I'm about to present my theory to the
uh, the uh, Senate, so that they can pass a law on
cruelty to lines, but uh, I'd just like to say this so
you can get an overall picture of, of the doom of
the world.

News

Chic: We are the newscasters, so just listen to what we have
to say, and remember, when we say you, we *mean*
you. Italy, which sat off the world market last week
in a blaze of pre-linguistic anarchy has been joined
there by the tiny but well-aimed country of Monaco,
which announced bankruptcy early today. Now a
feature from our own shores. Proceedings dragged on
today in the precedent-making grammar trials in
Kansas. Defense attorney Mr. Utah stated that the
charges of colloquialism and vagary brought against
his client were merely shrouding the vast body of
grammar crimes commited every day by the
American people without harrass.

Bab: I'd just like to say, Chic, that as the ebb and blow of
bi-sentinel, buy-american fervor is felt washing our
beaches there is a new awakening to the great grammatical
history of this great linguistic republic. Trials
such as this are springing up all over to test the tinsel
strength of our American language.

Station Identification

Bab: This is DOA, where you'll be seeing That's Those Faces, the new game show, later on tonight.

Commercial

Chic: *(fadeup)* Dexedron Central Drug Clearing House invites you to a big party! Tonight down at the warehouse by the old docks where the ships come rollin' in. . . Bring your I.D., get an idee of what drug clearing can do for you. Clear up to a thousand a week peddling drugs for our establishment. Yes kids, a one-in-a-lifetime invitation-only party. Just listen to what some of last year's members have to say.

Bab: *(reading)* I made over a hundred dollars in one week just selling these simple little Dexies.

Chic: You are guaranteed to wake up completely wasted after eight easy hours of the most refreshing clearing you have ever drugged.

Bab: Yes, drugs arent all bad, even though most of them are. But ours is good. Try it, sell some to your friends: remember, buying in quantity gives you an easy out if you're ever busted.
That's Dexedron, the clearing house of all variety.

Chic: Yes, you can make your own bail with Dexies.

Interview

Chic: Over the past few years, Americans in this country have been introduced to the thought and process of the mysticism of the East. This has particularly taken hold among the young people, who are now, in hordes, driving their parents insane in a grasping effort to reach Nirvana, one of the rewards that is promised by this. . . Eastern religion. So without further ado, I'd like to introduce a man who has been traveling around our country for the past five years, giving people insides into. . . just what he's doing in our country. so here is Mr. Yamahaamahama Gohotli Yoga.

Haami: *(a motley guru)* My brothers and sisters in the sister of the faithful good news, we give ourselves today for this humble blessing which we are about to be speaking from our Great Man up in the sky; shall we bow our heads for a moment of prayer: O man up in the sky, who gives us the great bread that falls out on our heads and sometimes put us out--

58

Chic: *(with eyes closed, trying to repeat)* O man up in the sky
            who gives us the great bread that falls out on our heads
            and makes us honest--

Haami: We give ourselves to thee for the divinity of thy own
            humble bread-baker--

Chic: We give ourselves over to thee for the enjoyment of
            our own humble bed-maker--

Haami: --and fall out on our knees in recompense to thy holy
            lemon juice--

Chic: --and fall out on our knees in reckless sense of our
            hauling lemming teeth--

Haami: *(flustered)* and find ourselves unable to reconcile our-
            selves to the knowledge that we cannot overcome our
            oatmeal--

Chic: --and are unable to reconcile ourselves to the knowledge
            that we might be pregnant--

Haami: And brothers and sisters in the faith who now--

Chic: Excuse me, Haami, we're going to have to do a comm-
            ercial break here so you're going to have to finish that
            prayer sometime later in the chapel.

Haami: O man in the sky dont let them bother you, we'll be
            right back.

Commercial

*(a kitchen set. A grubby child in pajamas is sitting on
the floor, pouting loudly.)*

Kid: Waaaaaaaaaaah!

Father: *(in hardhat and t-shirt, entering with a tray full of junk
            food)* Here, son, dive in! *(Kid begins to gobble foods.)*
            Y'know, my 18 year old pre-schooler wouldnt snack on
            anything but Junky Smack Foods. And I've learned
            over the years that you *can* skimp when it comes to
            your children, 'cause at that age, god they'll eat any-
            thing. That's why I'm glad there's Junky International.

Kid: I like it, it tastes good. There's Junky Potato Press
            Patties, Junky Pre-Chews, Choclet Junkys, Junky
            Twists, Junky Chopped Rhine-Squirrels, and a whole
            line of Junky Mashes, Sours, and Head Cheeses, Junk
            Mail, Junky Peanut Butter. . .

Father: Yes, my life is hectic enough without having to worry
            about what my kid is eating all day, so I'm glad the
            folks at Junky are doing it for me. And Junkys are

59

prefilled and labeled so I know it's good for him. So
the next time your kid pops his head up through the
floor and asks for more, dont panic! Just prop his
mouth open with a hefty tray of *Junk* Foods.
(blackout)

Chic: A random product of Junky International.

Interview Continued

Haami: *(fadeup)* --others and sisters who in the faith give you
our presence in the lord of our coming, we come upon
you with the golarious prentengitude to be humble
servants who cant speak a word of your language.
What do you say to this, lord?

Chic: *(amused)* Uh, could you speak right into this microphone over here?

Haami: *(still in trance)* I--I've never approached you so humbly.
Can we speak louder?

Chic: No, no, the angels are sleeping; it's nap time and the
milk truck hasnt arrived yet--our last shipment of milk
was filled with salt, and we're suing the commercial
broadcasters now.

Haami: Salt?. . . Broadcasters? . . .

Chic: *(snapping him out of it)* Haami, could you tell us a
little about what it is you're doing in our country?

Haami: Well, Chic, as you know I first came to this country 5
years ago to demonstrate the mind expending techniques
of transcendental meditation.

Chic: Yes, uh, well, what exactly is this . . . trans. . . trans-
fusional mediation. . . or whatever you called it?

Haami: Yes, well if you would just sit back and relax I'd be
happy to demonstrate.

Chic: All right, I'm sitting back now. . . My, you certainly
do look authoritative sitting there with your hair
flowing down and your beard flowing around, now
what should I do?

Haami: Just close your eyes and listen to what I have to say.
Picture yourself on a boat on a river. . . and after you've
done that, picture yourself on a groat with a cleaver. . .
and after you've done that, picture yourself as a tennis
racket going up against a ball. . . and after you've done
that picture yourself as a train, pulling into a station. . .
(faster) and after you've done that, picture yourself as

a badminton birdie, flying through the air. . . and
after you've done that, picture yourself as a cigarette,
going up in smoke. . . and after you've done that . . .
*(he continues faster and faster until his words and then
he is a blur, and at last he disappears.)*

Chic: Wow. . . he went away. . . I'm getting out of here. I
need a vacation just like half the other people around
this place. . . *(exit)*

Feature

Bab: Now we have a report sent in by our Baltimore corre-
spondent concerning some of the events of the last
week in Baltimore and surrounding areas. Chic, you
have that report?

Chic: Right, Bab. The great happening concerning Baltimore,
Maryland, this week didnt occur in Baltimore, Maryland,
but rather in Rome, Italy. Citizens of Baltimore,
Maryland, were there found lying in the gutter. This
greatly astounded Roman officials, so they revived
them and took them to the Rome Police Station. Upon
taking several hundred tests, it was found that these
young people, two from our benevolent state of
Baltimore--or of Maryland he must mean, you get a
little conceited when you live in the capital city--and
two from Puerto Rico, one of the U. S. possessions,
had been smoking marijuana. These people however
were not held in custody but were released on the
grounds that they couldnt understand. They then
went to a ballet and opera where they met two gentlemen from--also in the U. S. --Salt Lake City, Utah, and
there proceeded to stone them. They were not arrested
again, however they were surveilled. . . This surveillance
lasted for several days, until they left the country.
Right now we--or they--of Baltimore, Maryland, have
been faced with several such instances of this type, not
only in Rome, but in Florence, in Zurich, Switzerland,
in Munich, Germany, in Amsterdam, in Paris, in London,
everywhere people from Baltimore are getting ripped.

Bab: I understand several of the community leaders are
becoming quite concerned about this. We'll have a
televised panel discussion on this issue from Baltimore
tonight at ten, on DOA.

Chic: This is the DOA television network, where the newscasters give Damn Odd Arguments.

News

Bab: On the political scene, California Repugnican Elber Whisp today withdrew his bid for the Senate recall, seconds and thirds from his air force food locker, and the money from his bank account which has since propelled him to Uraguay, a footweary slowpoke in the international extinction race.

Chic: Whisp, a former Texas louse farmer and long time politician, said Uraguay would not fold, and quote, you can bet on that, unquote.

Bab: Coffee, Chic? Nelsewhere in the pews, farmers are picking Washington tomorrow to protest the lowering of the boom--er, ceiling--which has been skyhighed these last few months. Both native and American migrain workers have been giving their employers headaches with their seasonal demands for cost-of-living equity and, as one rancher put it, "all those stinking tents."

Chic: And speaking of seasoned workers, we'll be presenting a special news interpolation later tonight after we go off on migrain workers and what they eat: "We Like Em Fried--Kitchen Politics in Apricot City". Incidentally, Bab, how are those workers going to get home?

Bab: Well I dont know, Chic, but we do know they cant go to Canada.

Chic: That's right, Babyl, it's not there. *(blackout)*

Commercial

Chic: *(fadeup)* There's a lot of danger in the ordinary American house and one of the biggest killers is the common porcelain or cast iron bath tub. So to be sure nothing ugly happens to you when you're naked and unaware, here are a few tips to take:

Bab: When entering the tub, be sure all handles are fully operative. There should be six handles, two on each side, one on each end.

Chic: Before filling the tub, stick it to the rubber mat. Be
           safe, take at least three good laps on your feet, then
           sit and slide firmly with a circular motion.

Bab: Always have a friend or relative handy in the next room
           who can rush without embarrassment or hesitation to
           your aid at the slightest sound of disaster. Remember,
           it only takes a minute or two to drown, even less to
           electrocute, so please: dont forget these family re-
           minders brought to you by the Natural Home Bath
           Institute.

Feature-News-Interview

Bab: In the meantime, in between time, tonight's top story
           is coming to us direct from the Wide Hips of Doper
           where we have DOA sports plaintiff Bill Baytona's 500
           Lemmings and their famous race. Now I think we have
           Bill Daytona--uh, we switch you now to England and
           Bill Daytona.

Bill: *(via satellite)* Thank you, Chic. In all my 25 years of
           racing, I've never seen anything quite as marvelous as
           this. I convinced Chevrolet to bring out these 500
           Lemmings, and to have this exposition race--exhibition
           race--in which all the participants could drive their own
           cars. . . This is a remarkable effort on the part of
           Chevrolet to build up their declining sales quota, and
           . . . bolster my declining career.

Chic: How do you think the race will turn out, Bill, do you
           think the Lemmings will go over the cliff this time
           like last year or will there be a holdup due to contr-
           actual disease?

Bab: *(to Chic)* Delays.

Chic: Oh, delays.

Bill: Well, that's what I dont know. Ever since they put
           those locking steering wheels in, the little buggers just
           cant eat. Now it may lessen the chances of the cliffs
           holding up but definitely the cars *will* go over.

Bab: We understand there was a slight delay this morning
           before we brought our cameras out concerning a
           Lemming which had overboiled and spilled and caused
           several of the other Lemmings to sputter.

63

| Bill: | That's true. That's the major defect that they've built in to these Lemmings is that when one does it, they all do it. I just cant seem to get around it. . . They all *do* come with 4 wheels. . . Could you ask me another question?. . . |
| Chic: | Well, I'm afraid that's all the time we have, Bill, but we thank you for your report, and we'll be watching tomorrow to see how that race turns out. |

Closing

Chic:	It's that time, Bab.
Bab:	Yes, broadcasters, we've come to the end of another wonderful shift here at the helm of DOA Daytime. We hope you'll join us again tomorrow when we'll present another string of pearls gathered by our own divers methods.
Chic:	Of course we want to remind you that DOA continues with Nightime. So from America, this is Chic Uttley--
Bab:	And this is Babyl Snurr--
Unison:	Goodnight.

END

PILGRIM'S PROBLEMS

for the american bicentennial

characters:

"Granpa" Albert What, a janitor
"Ma" Miriam Taxpayer, his daughter
"Dad" Lou Taxpayer, her husband
Ralph, their son and grandson, a student
Dr. Woopie, a psychiatrist
Mr. Barney, Grandpa's boss
Larry, a friend of Ralph
students, fellow workers
the mayor

setting:

average american city, 1976

ACT I

scene I

(A residential street at night. We follow the sounds of crickets and cats in through a bedroom window where sleeps Granpa Albert What, fitfully. He wakes with a start.)

Granpa: *(shouting)* Logonite! Logonite! We must have logonite! *(in the family room, Ma, Dad, and Ralph are watching late night television.)*

Ma: Was that Granpa?

Ralph: We'd better go check on him.

Dad: I hope it's not logonauts again.
(They run to Granpa's room)

Granpa: We must have logonite! We must have logonite!

Dad: I am getting so sick of this dreaming I cant sleep anymore. Ma, we've got to do something about this.

Ralph: Dad, I told you a good piece of head shrinking would
do Granpa a world of good if he would agree to.

Ma: What you need is a big warm glass of milk Granpa, to
help you sleep and not have to dream.

Granpa: But we need logonite to worry no more about work or
money and not have disease. Logonite could save us,
I'm sure. C'mon Lou, say you'll go look with me, I--I--

Ma: You'll do nothing. You're just so overwrought these
days about your job and all and certainly none of us
is getting any younger but--

Ralph: Yeah, that's it. Granpa, your job will come back. Why,
thousands of aged cripples all over the country are
finding spaces in parking lots and all over the country--

Ma: Ralph, go back to bed or you'll be sick and I can see
to it.

Ralph: Aw, ma. . .*(exits)*

Dad: I think I'll go too. *(exits mumbling)* How we ever got
a lou-lou like that--lou-lou--no pun intended. . .

Granpa: Logonite logonite we must have logonite. Miriam, I
keep seeing it. The great logonite mine sustaining the
world and no more jobs. . .

Ma: Dad you always said jobs make the world go round,
but we all have to retire sometime and you can find
things to do, why it's the golden years you know, and
you can spend time with your grandchildren--

Granpa: Oh, I dont think Ralph likes me poking around in his
doings and anyway, I just cant keep up with these kids,
why at the school the little snots are cussin and talkin
about world going ons before they're 10.

Ma: We'll talk about it in the morning, dad. Would you
like some milk to help you sleep?

Granpa: No, no, it just makes my stomach white. I'll be okay.

Ma: Well, goodnight then. *(exit)*

Granpa: I'll be okay. Logonite. I could save the world with a
spade, renew its heart, no more clubs, more valuable
than diamonds. . . *(he sleeps)* *(blackout)*

scene 2

*(The kitchen of the Taxpayer home, next morning.
Ma is fixing breakfast, humming "it's a grand old flag".)*

Ma: *(loudly)* Lou! Get up! *(to herself:)* Discipline!

Ralph: *(trotting in)* Hi. When's Dad gonna get back some of his old vim and vinegar and start jogging down to breakfast everyday?

Ma: He just sleeps so bad every time after one of Granpa's dreams, and then he cant get awake in the morning. I wish your grandfather would get used to the idea that 69 is no fit age to still be working.

Ralph: Well, I dont know. . .

Ma: What?

Dad: *(entering)* Uhnhnhnhnhhh. . .

Ma: Here, have some wheat-darts to warm you up. Get the old blood circling.

Ralph: Hi, dad.

Dad: Hi, son. Going to school today?

Ralph: Sure dad, every tuesday.

Dad: Well, all I can say is you've got it a lot better than when I was a kid.

Ralph: Oh, I go other days too.

Dad: Oh, my neck. Miriam, where's the shortening?

Ma: Lou, you're short enough already, and all that's not good for you. I swear, you're as bad as Ralph, always gobbling up bad food.

Dad: Well, it makes me spry! If I could ever get a decent night's sleep. . .

Ralph: Hey yeah, where is Granpa? I want him to tell me his dream.

Ma: Ralph, I dont want you encouraging Granpa in this, he might fall down and hurt somewhere.

Dad: That's right, Ralph. Now, I like old people the same as the next guy, but we've got to stop this hullabaloulou.

Ralph: I still think Granpa needs a good shrink or somebody else who can really understand him. Like, this is more to him than just a dream, you know.

69

Dad: *(with newspaper)* Look at this. That League of Injustice
           Students is claiming another victory down at city hall.
           They've got a lot of skunk, those kids.

Ralph: They're not kids. They're real people. Students.

Ma: Ralph, now what do you know? And Lou, how can you
           talk that way about those young rebelrousers? Arent
           they the ones who defended that woman who used
           profanity?

Ralph: Ma, the ways of our lives are changing. You heard what
           Granpa said about the kids at his school.

Dad: Now I dont see anything wrong with a little profanity,
           but this LIS was defending it, Ralph.

Ralph: They're a good group, Dad.

Ma: Oh Ralphie!

Dad: Dont upset your mother.

Ma: It's too late. I feel the tears welling up inside me.
           Boohoo. Lou, turn the eggs.

Dad: Looks like they're dehydrated. I'll pick off a donut on
           the way to work. See you later everybody.

Ralph: Bye, Dad. What's the matter, Ma?

Ma: I just get so upset when I hear things about those
           LIS people trying to tear down our country.

Ralph: That's not true. Why, just look here in the paper:
           League of Injustice Students calls for halt to trailer
           discrimination.

Ma: What does that mean?

Ralph: Thousands of people who used to live somewhere else
           are stuck in trailers, and others who didnt, arent, dont
           you see--?

Ma: Ralph, our proud heritage began without anywhere to
           live and now it goes anywhere it likes, and first class,
           too. Why, I read in the Journal that america owns
           51% of the world--

Ralph: Oh, do you really believe that? The United Strates is
           a country with problems just like anybody--

Ma: What did you call it?

Ralph: What?

Ma: You called our country something. United Strates.

Ralph: I did?

Ma: I dont know why, but it sounds like something one of those Students would say.

Ralph: I--I must have heard it somewhere. It just slipped out.

Ma: Sometimes I wonder about you, Ralphie. . .
(Granpa enters)

Ralph: Oh, hi, Granpa.

Ma: Dad, you sit right down and let me warm your mouth.

Granpa: Ehyeah, I'm ready for a big breakfast.

Ralph: Hey Granpa, you wanna tell me about your dream?

Ma: Ralph!. . . Now, what you got to do today, Granpa?

Granpa: Why, I gotta go down to work.

Ma: Well, I thought you were going to see the doctor today.

Granpa: I gotta go see the school people about keepin my job.

Ma: Noooo! I made the appointment 3 weeks ago, to help you, Dad.

Ralph: You really think they'll keep you on, Granpa?

Granpa: I dont know. But I've got to do something--

Ma: --about those dreams! Dad, if you'd just let go like all the others, everything would be okay.

Granpa: But I havent done anytning. . .
(phone rings)

Ma: Oh. . . *(exit)*

Ralph: Tell me about your dream, Granpa. Did you get any closer to the mine?

Granpa: *(musing)* Dont know. Came to a big concrete thing. Couldnt get past.

Ralph: I sure wish I could help. With logonite around we wouldnt even need the LI-- *(Ma enters)* --how are the wheat-darts, Granpa?. . .

Granpa: What?

Ma: That was the doctor to remind us of your appointment. Now Dad, I dont want to have to worry, and I'll drive you down there, and I told him you hadnt forgotten.

Granpa: Okay, okay! Son, yr mother's been horsewhippin me into bein healthy since she was born. Doesnt seem to matter, though. . . still losin. . .

Ma: Now come on, Dad, here's your sweater. We've got to hurry. *(they exit)*

| Ralph: | Bye... Buy american. That's Ma. *(he walks to the phone and dials)* Hiya, kiddo! |

Ralph: Bye... Buy american. That's Ma. *(he walks to the phone and dials)* Hiya, kiddo!

Larry: *(on far end)* Is that you, Ralph?

Ralph: Course it's me. I gave the greeting didnt I?

Larry: Well, there's so many people starting to say that lately...

Ralph: I guess we better change it. Course you should know my voice by now.

Larry: Aw sure, I know you Ralph. Dont get excited.

Ralph: So where's the meeting?

Larry: Down by the docks at the warehouse... say, Ralph, I hear your Granpa's gonna have to kick off.

Ralph: Kick off?

Larry: Yeah, you know, retire?

Ralph: Oh, yeah, he's 69, and at the end of this school year they're gonna make him retire.

Larry: Hey, we oughta get the League on his case. That would be a real kick.

Ralph: Yeah, well we'll talk about it tonight.

Okay. About 7... *(blackout)*

scene 3

(A "shrink's office". Ma has just led Granpa in.)

Dr: *(leading Ma out)* Now you go on out and do some chopping Mrs. Taxpayer, and we'll call you when we're finished. Now then Mr. What. I'd like you to tell me about this dream of yours.

Granpa: You know about that?

Dr: Your daughter said a little.

Granpa: What does she know? She never listens to anything I say.

Dr: Mr. What, when did you begin to dream?

Granpa: Why, when I was a little kid, right off.

Dr: No, I mean this dream about the logonate mine?

Granpa: It's logonite. And its hidden in the ground. Close to the surface. All we got to do is mine it and the world will be a garden again.

Dr: When did you first decide this?

Granpa: I didnt. It decided me. I mean, when I first knew I had to retire. It was like a vision. Clear. Shiny. Manageable...

Dr: Then you know where this mine is?

Granpa: No, I--

Dr: You dont know where it is?

Granpa: Yes, I--

Dr: Mr. What, how old are you?

Granpa: 69. Not too old I've got fire still water runs deep. . .

Dr: I just cant see how a man with the mileage you've got could believe such a thing like this.

Granpa: Somebody has to. World needs logonite. No more work. Just mine it once. All problems solved. No war. No work. No countries.

Dr: No countries?! Why Mr. What--ah, may I call you Albert?

Granpa: My name is Albert.

Dr: Exactly. Now Albert, countries are what the world is all about.

Granpa: No, no, countries make wars, jobs. . .

Dr: Jobs. Hmmm. You seem pretty worried about yours. Could it be you've made up this logonite because you're disappointed about your job?

Granpa: Not disappointed. Must work. No. Must find logonite. . . got to go look. . . *(he starts to leave)*

Dr: Just a minute, Albert. Now listen. Everybody has a dream they wish to work for, and I want to help you--

Granpa: Oh good, got to go look. Maybe the park. . .

Dr: I want to help you find a dream that's real. Something you can love and work for--

Granpa: *(shouting)* I love logonite! I got no time for this. Got to find it. *(opens door)*

Dr: Where are you going Albert?

Granpa: Got to meet boss. . . keep job. . . no time. . .*(exit)*

Dr: Albert, you're so confused.
            (blackout)

(The City School Board building. Office of Granpa's boss. Granpa enters timidly.)

Granpa: Mr. Barney?

Boss: Oh, hello Albert, come in come in sit down sit down now what can I do for you?

Granpa: It's about my job, I--

Boss: Well, that's all taken care of. After monday, no work, time to get old quietly. . .

Granpa: No, I want to work. Till I can find logonite at least.

Boss: Now Albert, we've been through this before. You're well past the school board's regular retirement age already. You've got to retire. A man of your age, still being a janitor, why you might fall down and hurt somewhere.

Granpa: But the kids. They tear up the bathrooms, clay all over, papers, without me such a mess, what would they do?

Boss: Well Albert, I'm sure we can find someone who after they learn the ropes could maybe someday get as good as you. . .

Granpa: By the way, could you order 200 feet of rope? Got to get those outside windows washed this summer. So much to do. Summer's the time. The school needs me. Get it fixed up for fall. . . kids come back. . . fresh. . . teachers smile at me. . . jokes. . .

Boss: Yes Albert, you're a good custodian. Maybe the best. And we depreciate you. But now its time for us to do something for you. Why, we want you to have fun with your family, get some rest--

Granpa: I'm not tired. . .

Boss: Oh, I think you are. And you'll find lots to do you've wanted to do all your life and waited for. . .

Granpa: I'll find logonite.

Boss: Yes, well, I'm sure. Now you let us know if we can do anything and--just between you and me -- I think some of the teachers are planning a little dinner or something for you the last day of school. . .
(blackout)

scene 5

*(On the city sidewalks a few minutes later. Granpa
walks along, mumbling.)*

Granpa: Didnt believe me. Nobody does. But they need me. If
I could convince. . . the mayor. He's old. He'd under-
stand. Went to school with him . . .
(Ralph enters walking from other way.)

Ralph: *(mumbling)* --scrap em here and take em there and get a
new look at-- Oh, hi Granpa.

Granpa: No, Ralphie, low. . .

Ralph: Huh?

Granpa: Two quarts low.

Ralph: Oh, they wouldnt give you your job back huh?

Granpa: No. No work, no logonite. . .

Ralph: Gee, Granpa, I'd like to help you. . . wait a minute.
Maybe I can.

Granpa: Huh?

Ralph: See ya later, Granpa. *(exit)*

Granpa: Oh, yeah, thanks Ralph, I always did like that boy. . .
(blackout)

scene 6

*(A warehouse. 20 or 30 young people are gathering.
Ralph and Larry enter, conversing.)*

Ralph: Hey you know, that idea of yours about Granpa wasnt
as funny as I thought.

Larry: Well, sure man, go ahead and bring it up tonight. You're
the only one that ever talks anyway. *(he claps his hands.)*
This meeting of the League of Injustice Students is now in
order. . . in order that our illustrated secretary-general can
bring up his dinner--I mean, an idea for us. Go ahead,
Ralph.

Ralph: Folks, we've been making noise about students for awhile
now, trying to make it easier for the average young dipper
to make a break of it in this organization minded society.
Our league is now recognized by most of the city leaders
as a real force and we really are. We are real, and we

really have caused a commotion in the civic government.
Now we all agree that students and foreigners have been
given a runaround for their whole trip and we're tired
of being treated like children and I think they're going
to stop. But now, I want to speak for another group
of children: the old people. Yes, there are a lot of
them in our area, old folks who dont know when to say
no or why to say yes. I have one in my house, you all
probably do too, or will someday. These old people
have no one to speak for them and one by one they are
being shelved like worn out novels we've read too many
times. My Granpa is one of these trusty old books and
I'm here to ask your help, the League's help, to help
him. See, my grandfather works for the school board
and, well for some strange reason he doesnt want to retire.
He's 4 years over the age now and at the end of this
school year they're going to make him retire. Now
granted it's not been our policy to express any interest
in jobs as a meaningful form of endeavor, and we
certainly dont want anyone to hear us coming right
out and saying jobs is good per se; but I think we have
a special parallel relationship you might say with the
old people, if we would just approach them, and I'd
like us to take up Granpa What's case as our next League
Lean. Seeing him like I do everyday, wanting to keep
working, fearing for his life almost, he's even starting
to have success fantasies. I--I--well, you all know Granpa
What, he cleaned up our school for us all through our
elementary years, and I think with the power we're
starting to wield we could help him and make a

spectacle besides, and really lean on city hall!

Larry: Right on!
             (blackout)

scene 7

(The Taxpayer home. Dad and Ma are watching tv.)

Ma: Lou, where is Ralph so late?

Dad: *(distracted)* So long. Gone. I dont know.

Ma: Lou, I worry about him.

Dad: Oh. . .

Ma: Dad, you're as bad as Granpa, you never listen to me.

Dad:	Huh, well I'll be damned.
Ma:	If only he'd cut his hair.
Dad:	Look at this headline, Miriam. "LIS Asks What About What. Activist group seeks job rebate."
Ma:	What? What?
Dad:	No, What. Your father. This LIS group is making an issue out of his retirement.
Ma:	Oh no.
Dad:	Yeah, listen to this: "Spokesman for the LIS said today that old people should have all the right to work they want. The secretary-general of the LIS who asked to remain anonymous, said old pokes in a society of wish fulfill society should have every opportunity to drink from the well while the bucket is up."
Ma:	You mean they want him to keep working? I hoped this would all bowl over and then maybe Granpa would stop those aweful dreams.
Dad:	Nothing'll stop that except a good clout on the head. What I want to know is, how the LIS got in on this.
Ma:	Lou, I'm worried about Ralphie.
Dad:	He'll be in in awhile.
Ma:	No, I mean. . . do you think it's possible he's been talking to some of those radical Leaguers?. . . *(blackout)*

ACT II

scene 1

(The office where Lou Taxpayer works, the next morning. When Lou enters, his co-workers being to, as they say, give him a hard time.)

Dad:	Morning boys.
1st co:	Hey Lou, I see where yr father-in-law is gettin mixed up with that League of Injustice Stupids.
Dad:	Well ah. . .
2nd co:	Yeah, mixed up is right, ha ha! Look at this in this morning's paper. "We are going to find Iogonite, a marvelous mineral which will save humans from themselves." Ha ha, what do ya make a that?

Dad: Oh no. . .

1st co: Yeah, Ha ha, he must be as crazy as those kids!

Dad: He's got this crazy dream of logonite--

2nd co: I wonder why they picked old Albert for their puppet
            this time. Seems like they're really trying to start
            trouble in your house, Lou. Ha ha ha.

Dad: Dont you try to start trouble in my house.

1st co: Hey Lou, yr boy Ralph ever talk to any of those LIS
            people?. . .

scene 2

*(A residential street. Granpa is walking along the
sidewalk toward home, musing to himself.)*

Granpa: O de doe, la de da, lo-go-nite, cha cha cha. . .

Ralph: *(coming alongside)* Hiya kiddo--I mean, Granpa.

Granpa: Hi Ralph.

Ralph: What did Ma's shrink have to tell ya?

Granpa: I'm crazy.

Ralph: Huh. A lot he knows. By the time we finish with
            your case, nobody'll know you're crazy.

Granpa: My case?

Ralph: Listen, The league had a meeting, and I told them how
            you had to retire, and they decided to make it a project
            to get your job back.

Granpa: The. . . League?

Ralph: *(confidentially)* Yeah, you know. The League of
            Injustice Students.

Granpa: Oh, oh, dont let your mother find out, she'd mop
            the floor with you. . .

Ralph: Not a chance, we're all anonymous.

Granpa: That's wonderful, Ralph, you're going to wield the
            broom and dustpan for me?

Ralph: That's right Granpa. Tonight the League is going to
            march on the steps of city hall. . .
            *(suddenly they are standing before city hall, the LIS
            and a crowd of people gathered around. Ralph's voice
            becomes amplified.)*
            . . .and get that job back that he fully deserves! Albert

78

What is a good american, with a dream for all of us;
who wants to work for the people of this city, unlike
some of the community leaders--

Mayor: *(storming up to the microphone)* Just a minute!

Ralph: --like the mayor--

Mayor: This dream, this incredible dream!

Ralph: What?

Mayor: Are you trying to make a laughing stock of this
government?

Ralph: *(trying to address the people)* Mr. Mayor, he has a
right--

Mayor: To make up this logonite story? He's crazy!

Granpa: But we need logonite so we dont have to work and
have no more disease.

Mayor: I thought you wanted to work!

Ralph: Logonite is Granpa's idea of a world where work isnt
needed anymore. Dont you see?

Mayor: Sure I do. Your Granpa is a dreamer and you're a fool.
Ha! *(exits muttering)* What a bunch of snorting. . .
*(The crowd laughs and begins to ridicule Ralph, Granpa,
and the LIS, then all the spectators begin to walk off.)*

Larry: Hey Ralph, you blew it.

Marry: Everybody's leaving.

Harry: They may never take us seriously again.

Ralph: Oh wow. . .
(blackout)

scene 3

*(The living room, late evening. Ma and Dad are
sitting.)*

Dad: I'll talk to Ralph when he comes in and one way or
another, we'll get this whole thing straightened out, I
promise you that.

Ralph: *(entering despondently)* Hi.

Dad: Sit down son, we want to talk to you.

Ralph: I'm kinda tired Dad.

Ma: This is important.

Dad: Ralph, you know how your mother and I have wanted
you to become a medical major in college, and when you

79

failed to do that in the appropriate time we naturally
became worried as you can well expect. Now dont you
think you have some responsibility to us; after all, we're
financing your way through college.

Ralph: Dad, all the other kids, they dont have to work or any-
thing--

Ma: That's no excuse. Just because your father works hard
and gives you a good allowance so you dont have to
work and have more time to study, that's no reason
to go ahead and do what you want. You have a responsibility to your father who's paying for your
schooling.

Ralph: Aw Ma, I went down to the malt shop the other day
to study, but all those kids down there. . . you cant
expect me to forsake my social reputation just for
the sake of a little education.

Dad: Son, I know how you feel, but look--we all had to
buckle under once to get where we are now. If I hadnt
done that once you probably wouldnt have been born;
if I hadnt gone to school I wouldnt have met your
mother--

Ralph: All my life I've been filling out forms, putting down
my name under yours. Where do I fit into this picture?
I'm not just an extension--I have my own dial.

Dad: That's right. Luckily for you, we're above the average
level of wealth for our society; but if your mother and
I hadnt been married you would have been illegitimate
and this would be a very much different problem.

Ralph: Mom, Dad, look, all I want to do is get a car and a girl
and find some place to--

Dad: That's the spirit, son! That's what college can get you.
Now you study hard and one of these weekends we'll
jump in the car and drive down to the beach and pick
up a couple of girls and--

Ma: What?

Ralph: Dad!

Dad: Er, uh, well, you got to have a little fun in college. . .

Ralph: But I want you to pay me more money to go. I want
you to pay me enough, so that when I graduate, I dont
have to work for the rest of my life.

Dad: Do you expect me to just dole out money to you?

Ma: Oh Ralphie, there's so much to pay for, with the rising
           costs and inflation; why just the other day I was in the
           store and eggs were 75 cents a dozen, and I can remember
           the day not more than 2-3 months ago when eggs were
           48 cents a dozen. Now you dont realize how hard your
           father has to work. He's down there sometimes from
           7 in the morning till 9 at night; and just because you
           spend half your time away from home and dont have
           to listen to him come home and nag at me anymore is
           no reason that you should get so up out of ordinary
           kilter over this money situation. Didnt you make any
           money all summer what happened did you spend all
           your money on what??

Ralph: Mom, I've got the habit.

Ma: What habit, son?! Talk to me, I'm your mother!

Ralph: I have the habit of spending money, Ma. Drugs take
           so much. . . girls take so much. . .

Ma: Drugs! Oh!. . . Girls! Oh!. . .

Ralph: It's only one part of it, you know? Like, I spend some
           money on books, too.

Dad: Son, you got something to tell us? I get the feeling
           there's something going on here that we havent been
           let in to know about.

Ralph: That's true. I've been spending a lot of money on
           doctor bills.

Dad: Doctor bills? What've you got to go to a doctor for,
           young healthy kid like you, eighteen, nineteen, how
           old are you now, twenty?

Ralph: I'm 21, Dad, I'm an adult now.

Dad: Son, you shouldnt be going to a doctor so often, what
           you got to go to a doctor for?

Ralph: Well, I thought I might be pregnant.

Ma: Oh, son!

Ralph: But I'm not. Dont worry, Dad. Ma, calm down.

Dad: Thank god!

Ma: Son, why didnt you tell us, we could have got you a
           good obstetrician.

Ralph: Well, I've been hoping to change my sex, and these
           operations cost money--

Dad: Son! What did you say? Change what?

Ralph: *(hedging)* Change?. . .Oh, change my major. . . I dont
            want to go into obstetrics; I want to go into golf.

Dad: Son, obstetrics is where you r uncle went into and look
            where it got him. If he hadnt died early and given it all
            to his nephew Eddie you would have gotten it all, but
            instead I decided to make sure you were gonna be an
            obstetrics major in college because I know when you
            go to college you can really get good at something and
            obstetrics is really a good way to make money. Now,
            money is where it's at, son, and whether you realize it
            or not some day you're gonna find it out. And you
            just listen to your mother when she talks about groc-
            eries because for nigh on to, uh, 21 years now I've been
            supporting you, except for when you went away to
            college and got into all those bad habits.

Ralph: Come on, I was into those bad habits before college,
            Dad.

Ma: Aaah--*(she faints)*

Ralph: Ma!

Dad: Now son, I want you to tell me exactly what you meant
            by that.

Ralph: Ma's passed out.

Dad: Good, she wont have to hear what I think you're about
            to say. We're alone now, and you can tell me, man to
            man.

Ma: *(reviving)* Uhnhnnnn. . . my goodness.

Dad: Ah. . . shit.

Ralph: Well Dad, she has a right to hear!

Ma: Hear what?

Ralph: Well, I ah. . .

Dad: He's about to tell us the truth about himself.

Ralph: The truth?

Ma: Well, I'm all for that. America was built on truth.

Dad: Ralph, do you know anything about how the LIS got
            onto Granpa's case?

Ralph: Well, I--

Ma: Come on, Ralphie dear, we want to hear.

Ralph: Ma, you're asking for it.

Dad: You're damn right we're asking for it! Now stop double-talking me and start straighttalking me!

Ralph: Well. . . you know that anonymous secretary-general who made the statements on t.v.?

Ma: Yes?. . .
(a heavy pause)

Dad: You?

Ralph: That's right.

Ma: God help us.

Dad: Well, I always said you'd be a leader, but--

Ma: Ralphie how could you? Say it isnt true.

Ralph: It's true.

Ma: I feel like I might faint. . .

Ralph: *(jumping up)* Here, lie down.

Dad: Dont touch her!

Ralph: What?

Dad: Well, I, hurumph, er. . .

Ralph: You okay, Ma?

Ma: Has all my effort been in vain? Dont you love our country?

Ralph: Well sure I do. I just dont want to see it become more important than people in general. And besides, I dont see why you guys dont want to help Granpa, too.

Dad: Dont change the subject. Why of all the--you're in the LIS!

Ralph: Yes! Now if we're never gonna get past that point I dont want to talk anymore.

Dad: Well, what do you suggest, Ralph?

Ralph: How about what this country means to you and why you never want to change anything?

Ma: What do you mean "change"?

Ralph: You forget what "change" means?

Dad: Now dont be disrespectful to your mother.

Ralph: I'm only trying to point out that we need change, and the LIS--

Ma: *(hysterically)* They're nothing but rebelrousers, the way they march around city hall and the capitol building.

Ralph: That's me you're talking about.

Ma: Ohhhhh. . . . *(she crys)*

Dad: That's enough Ralph. We'll talk about this later. Come
           on, mother, it's time for bed.

Ralph: But--

Dad: I said that's enough! Cant you see your mother is too
           upset? *(they exit)*

Ralph: *(stunned)* Wow. . . how ridiculous. . . how absurd.
           *(He walks slowly to the back door and out into the
           back yard. It is late. Granpa is sitting on a step,
           fingering old dead leaves from the ground.)*
           Hi, Granpa.

Granpa: Morning.

Ralph: Well, not quite. . . I guess they really punched us out
           this time, huh?

Granpa: Yeah, punched us up. Cant understand.

Ralph: Yeah. . . you sleepy?

Granpa: My life, all my life. . . no.

Ralph: I thought they'd listen to us. We've done it before.
           But all they wanted to talk about was logonite. That
           wasnt even the real issue.

Granpa: We must find logonite, Ralphie.

Ralph: I know, Granpa, it's a good dream.

Granpa: Oh, they'll never believe me.

Ralph: It's okay, we can still fight for your job. It's a setback,
           sure, but--

Granpa: Ralphie. . . *(he pulls out a letter)*

Ralph: Hey, that's from your boss.

Granpa: Letter from the school board. I'll read it to you.
           What?. . . Oh, "What: The retirement board of the
           board of ed hereby denies renewal of your employment
           by said board. Will be pleased to receive you no later
           than June 3 for refreshments and farewell reception."

Ralph: Oh no. . .

Granpa: We lost. Came hoppin up too fast and surprised em
           and they cut us down.

Ralph: I'm sorry, Granpa. I really blew the whole thing. I just got carried away. I got so involved with issues that I forgot about real people.

Granpa: I could have worked, and lived. . . I was alive.

Ralph: Hey, listen. You and I can understand each other, Granpa. Dad and Ma cant understand; they have too much to lose. But we dont have anything to lose. Dont have any jobs. And you're gonna be around for a long time, Granpa.

Granpa: These. . . these leaves were living. . . living leaves. . . and green. . . and veiny with food. . . and now they're oh so troubled. . .

Ralph: But it'll be okay, Granpa. I mean, we're young and old with a rubber consistency. Right?

Granpa: Right, Ralph. Just because you didnt see it, doesnt mean it wasnt there.

CURTAIN

Ralph: I'm sorry, Stamford. I really like the whole thing. I just
          got involved now. I guess involved with issues that

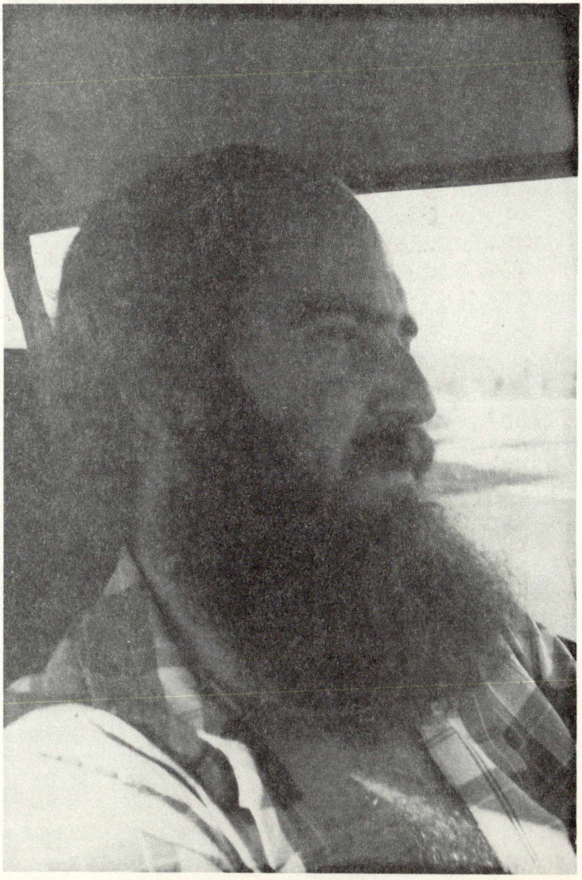

Litmus first editions r edited by Charles Potts and published by Litmus Inc., a non-profit corporation, Reverend Sherm W. Clow, President.

karen waring	*exposed to the elements*	2.00
greg stewart & nolan palmer	*the refillable steamy*	3.00
edward smith	*going*	2.00
	the flutes of gama	3.00
kell robertson	*all the bar room poetry in this world can't mend this heart of mine, dear*	1.00
charles potts	*th golden calf*	4.00
	the opium must go thru	2.00
jo merrill	*waterweed*	2.00
richard krech	*the incompleat works of richard krech, poems 1966-1974*	3.00
peter koch	*magnus annus*	1.00
david hiatt	*vanish*	1.50
charley george	*a more*	2.00
charles foster	*peyote toad*	2.00
mike finley	*lucky you*	2.00
andy clausen	*extreme unction*	2.00
charles bukowski	*poems written before jumping out of an 8 story window*	3.00

| charles foster | *victoria mundi clothbound from smith/horizen/litmus nyc* | 4.50 |